P9-BYX-936

Crossing Cultural Borders: Education for Immigrant Families in America

Crossing Cultural Borders: Education for Immigrant Families in America

Concha Delgado-Gaitan
and
Henry Trueba

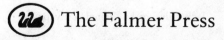 The Falmer Press

(A member of the Taylor & Francis Group)
London · New York · Philadelphia

UK   The Falmer Press, Rankine Road, Basingstoke, Hampshire RG24 0PR

USA   The Falmer Press, Taylor & Francis Inc., 1900 Frost Road, Suite 101, Bristol, PA 19007

© C. Delgado-Gaitan and H.T. Trueba, 1991

All rights reserved. No part of this publication may be reproduced, stored in a retrieval system, or transmitted, in any form or by any means, electronic, mechanical, photocopying, recording, or otherwise, without permission in writing from the Publisher.

First published 1991

British Library Cataloguing in Publication Data
Delgado–Gaitan, Concha
Crossing cultural borders: education for immigrant families in America.
1. United States. Immigrant children. Education
I. Title II. Trueba, Henry T.
371.9700973

ISBN 1–85000–885–X
ISBN 1–85000–886–8 pbk

Library of Congress Cataloging-in-Publication Data
Delgado-Gaitan, Concha.
    Crossing cultural borders: education for immigrant families in America/Concha Delgado-Gaitan and Henry Trueba.
    p. cm.
    Includes bibliographical references and index.
    ISBN 1-85000-885-X: — ISBN 1-85000-886-8 (pbk.):
    1. Socialization.   2. Hispanic American children.
3. Hispanic Americans — Cultural assimilation.   4. Hispanic American children — Education.   5. Home and school — United States. I. Trueba, Henry T. II. Title.
HQ783.D44   1991
305.2′3′08968073 — dc20   90-40815
                                            CIP

Jacket design by Benedict Evans

Typeset in 12/14 Bembo by
Graphicraft Typesetters Ltd, Hong Kong

Printed in Great Britain by Burgess Science Press, Basingstoke

305.23
D378c

Contents

Dedication and Acknowledgments

We dedicate this book to the families of Secoya. We also dedicate this book to the children in our families in recognition of the many things they have taught us: affection, enthusiasm, trust, desire to learn and candor. Therefore, these pages are for Mark Phillip, Nicole, April, Andrea, Anitra, and Thomas; and for Laura Jean and Phillip Henry. We wish to express our gratitude to all our colleagues in the Council of Anthropology and Education, and those involved in Educational Anthropology, Sociology and Psychology whose work has inspired our research efforts.

The stimulating ideas of Paulo Freire, G. Peter Murdock, George DeVos, George and Louise Spindler, Marcelo Suárez-Orozco, Frederick Erickson, David Smith, Perry Gilmore and many others, have found their way in our overall conceptualization of the ethnography of empowerment and our data analysis. May these thoughts be our gift to them. We also wish to thank our students and staff who helped us generously: Vincent De Young, Mary Kimber, Hector Mendez, Mary Alice Flint, and Mimi Navarro. Without their diligent efforts this book would have never been completed. We also want to extend our gratitude to Carmen Delgado-Contreras of the Bilingual Education Office, County of San Mateo, for the valuable information provided on the Secoya community. Additionally we appreciate the support received from the Academic Senate of the University of California, Santa Barbara, and from the Division of Education at the University of California, Davis.

Dedication and Acknowledgments

Most of all the authors want to thank the wonderful families of the 'Secoya' (pseudonym). Parents, children, community leaders and friends opened their homes and their hearts to us without expecting anything in return. It was their voices in Spanish, their struggles and dreams that found an English expression through our writing.

Preface: An Ethnography of Empowerment

The ethnographic study of minority groups in plural societies has gained increasing momentum in the past three decades. The pages of the leading publications in education, mental health and the field of justice increasingly rely on the technographic findings of anthropologists and others to confront the problems facing ethnic minorities in complex societies. The study of schooling as an institution of society is of immense policy importance given its complex relationships with issues such as unemployment and underemployment rates, delinquency rates and other key indexes of social anomie and psychological alienation. This new study by Concha Delgado-Gaitan and Henry T. Trueba is in the best tradition of the field of anthropology and education.

We must note that these issues are no longer uniquely American preoccupations. For example, Western European scholars are increasingly scrutinizing questions of comparative ethnicity as Europe contends with the issues of unification and the occupational and social future of second and third generation children of immigrants from the Mediterranean world living in Northern Europe.

Although the field of educational anthropology is a relatively new specialization within the broader subfield of sociocultural anthropology, comparing the developments in ethnographic research among ethnic minorities in the US and Europe will become of import to the history of anthropology. The study of the anthropology of education grew in the shadow of its older cousins, psychological anthropology and anthropological linguistics. Psychological anthropology has been influencing the field of anthropology and education most notably by attracting some its finer minds including George and Louise Spindler (Delgado-Gaitan's and Trueba's mentors) among others.

Any history of anthropology and education, therefore, must fully consider the impact of psychological anthropology via its empirical studies of socialization as a form of enculturation or cultural transmission. Additionally, the specific field of linguistic anthropology, particularly the study of the relationships between language, cognition, and society has also made singular contributions to the field of education.

Anthropologists now consider the school in society as a key institution taking over certain socialization tasks which in simpler societies were typically the responsibility of the kin group. Yet it has been only in the last three decades that a distinct subfield of anthropology and education can be identified with its own scholarly literature, special journals and annual meetings. The comparatively late arrival of this subfield can be traced to the central concerns of both American and European anthropologists favoring the study of isolated, 'traditional' societies, relatively 'uncontaminated' by Western and modern influences. There was need to record 'native culture', before the advancing modern world would forever change it. Franz Boas' efforts among the Pacific Northwest Coast Indians, for example, were in part motivated by this urgency to record learned patterns of native art and artisanship, social structure, mythology, economic exchange, etc., before they were altered by the encroaching modern world.

Anthropologists generally worked in technologically simpler societies *without* institutions of formal schooling as understood in the Western world. Typically, in these societies socialization was primarily the responsibility of the kin group. Increasing technological complexity lengthened the period between childhood and adulthood giving relatively recent birth to a concept of 'adolescence' as a specific stage in the life cycle. Technologically simple societies traditionally had no schools nor did they have adolescents: only boys, girls, men and women.

Schools particularly rose as formal institutions bridging the increasing gap between childhood and full adulthood.

When Western-style schools did appear in simpler societies, the early anthropologists selectively avoided study of them. It was the view of many early anthropologists that these new institutions simply represented the introduction of Western culture modifying native traditions.

The Post Colonial World

A number of important developments affected the character of anthropology as it is practiced in a post-colonial period. Anthropologists today are increasingly turning inward, examining their own societies, finding that the idea of culture, the dominant idea in modern anthropology, applies well to the study of ethnic problems in modern complex systems.

Anthropologists are not as welcome in the post-colonial world. Second, scholars from outside the Western cultural tradition are themselves becoming anthropologists, offering their own readings of 'native' cultures. Third, anthropology's 'former natives' (in current post-modern parlance 'the Other') have become a substantial and enduring feature in the inner cities of the more powerful wealthier centers of the North in Europe and the US. Today our cities have become ever more complex as peoples of the former colonies (now called the 'third' and 'fourth' worlds) migrated North and closed the colonial and dependency circle. As those studying inner cities in the US and Western Europe can attest, immigrant minorities are part of a more interdependent and complex ethnic world than the founders of the discipline of anthropology could have anticipated.

The post-war era in the United States and Europe has indeed witnessed migrants and refugees from the 'peripheries' or 'developing' world continuing to infiltrate the wealthier centers of the North in search of a better tomorrow for themselves and, most importantly, for their children. In addition to the previous waves of migrants into the US is the most recent surge of Hispano immigration. Hispanos are now the second largest minority group in the US. With a fertility rate about 60 per cent higher than the non-Hispano average and due to continuing immigration from Mexico, Central and South America, Hispanos are the fastest-growing minority group in the US. Soon they will numerically surpass Blacks as the nation's largest minority group. Asians are also entering in increasing numbers and are changing the demographic mix, particularly in the West Coast.

In a similar fashion, Europe, traditionally a continent of emigration and not immigration, has seen important population changes since the Second World War. It is now estimated that by the beginning of the twenty-first century, almost one-third of the population under the age of 35 in urban Europe will be of immigrant background. We must emphasize that these immigrants did not sneak in overnight, unnoticed or unwelcome. In the US, the so-called *bracero* program encouraged the entry of seasonal migrant workers from Mexico. Likewise in Europe, in many cases, the post-war immigrants were actively recruited by powerful sectors of the very Northern European countries that now fact an 'immigrant problem'. In the process, these immigrants became 'minorities,' and created a new uneasiness about the 'foreigners' in European and US cities.

Anthropologists in the developed world now face in their own backyards the kinds of problems they used to travel long journeys to decipher. These new problems include fascinating economic and social patterns. Today remittances from the immigrant minorities living in the wealthier Northern region literally feed billions of dollars into the peripheries. In the US case, for example, it has been estimated that Salvadorean refugees sent during the mid-1980s an average of 400 to 600 million dollars in remittances back to their troubled homeland. The same general pattern applies to Hispano immigrants from Mexico.

US and European psychologists, educators and sociologists as well as anthropologists are increasingly relying on ethnographic approaches in their studies of ethnic minorities. The new commitment to research in this area is surely motivated not only by 'pure' intellectual curiosity. Rather, it seems to be fueled by a growing concern that what happens in the adaptation to schooling among the descendants of the new immigrants will surely be an important determinant of the kind of future society that shall emerge. In Europe the questions include: will Europe become what the Council of Europe in one official document has called a 'segregated' society practicing 'apartheid'? Or will there develop a better atmosphere of interethnic harmony and respect based on democratic participation?

The School as a Multi-Ethnic Institution

What is going on with children in the school environment is a good place to start trying to understand the issues facing ethnic minorities. It is precisely in schools of the majority culture where many of the problems of some ethnic minorities begin or intensify. The emergence of countercultural gangs, the problem of deviancy and delinquency formation among minority youths are arguably the most serious and destructive sequelae of early non-learning and failure in school.

In the US, scholars have been pursuing such questions for some time. In this volume, Concha Delgado-Gaitan and Henry T. Trueba probe issues of learning in the home and in school, ethnic empowerment and democratic participation in an American setting with scientific rigor and empathic understanding.

In the US the problem of school functioning among ethnic minorities is hardly a recent development. Already over a century ago there were premonitions that certain key problems in minority education, heatedly debated today would be difficult to resolve. It is unnerving to think that the problem of ethnic variability in educational adaptation, with some immigrant minorities doing brilliantly in schools and others doing poorly was already evident over a century ago.

By their own careful, sensitive ethnographic studies, Henry Trueba and Concha Delgado-Gaitan have been adding notably to the many current theoretical contentions about the school adaptation of minorities. In this instance, focusing on Hispano children in one US community in the Southwest, they discuss what is more readily applicable to the problems of schooling in respect to all ethnic and social divisions presently operating. By ethnographic observation they skillfully document the role of culture in determining patterns of learning, whether in the school or at home. Their purpose is not a simple description of what is, but how possibly to use objective knowledge to instigate ameliorative intervention.

The survival and broadening of American democracy depends on raising the educational achievement and economic attainments of the new wave of immigrants, as well as improving the educational and economic attainments of those in every segment of our society whatever their past origin. This volume is addressed to that goal.

The authors enter directly into why there has been so high a rate of failure, or poor utilization of the vocational and general possibilities of American public education by specific minorities. What are the complex relationships between culture, minority status, educational outcomes and economic attainment across groups? Is, simply, class background the answer, as Marxist-oriented scholars have been advocating? Is it the prime mover in the educational achievement and eventual economic attainment of children? Or, conversely, is it culture, particularly as it shapes a work ethic, or its opposite, a 'culture of poverty'? Or, is it a matter of language and other cultural discontinuities between groups coming in contact? The questions are many and the stakes are high. Delgado-Gaitan and Trueba directly dispute any simple culture 'deficit' theory to explain failure.

Community Empowerment and School Policy

Empirically oriented, this volume seeks to acquaint us up close with the daily activities and experiences of children, the social and personal *meaning* of daily life in which school attendance is but one part. How do parents interact with children in respect to school? What continuities and discontinuities are experienced in interaction as the children move from the minority home culture to the majority school setting? Poverty, linguistic limitations and lack of knowledge of the social patterns of the majority population influence the child's world. They limit or prevent parents from feeling part of the system in which the school operates, or is supposed to operate.

How do the parents themselves learn about American society? How do these Hispano children, as the children of all immigrants, manage to bridge the home culture and the majority culture? And what governs their relative receptivity to new norms? The comprehension of how to operate in a democracy depends on some realization that one can have input; more than that, on the realization that one *must* have input, rather than remaining a passive object. An awareness of being a subject, a possible initiator of action needs to be awakened. If some lack the necessary knowledge on how to do something, there must be put into place some system whereby the individual or group is helped to understand, and afforded the means to learn how to cause things to happen.

Of notable theoretical significance is what might be termed the structure or 'grammar' of the empowering process perceptively identified and described by Delgado-Gaitan and Trueba. How does parental involvement ignite a process of empowerment? What are the changes parents undergo in the various stages of the empowerment process? How does this impact the children? A *sine qua non* in the process of empowerment is the emergence of an awareness in individual parents of a *common* history of social isolation. A new consciousness about the shared nature of specific problems subverts a sense of isolation and helplessness. As parents begin to share with one another their mutual problems they also build a consciousness of their rights and responsibilities. As the old Spanish proverb has it, *la unión hace la fuerza* (join and conquer). Parents mobilize for further community support confronting their old fears with a new sense of resolution to form organizations to have direct input into the schooling of children. Parents thus gain a voice; they must be heard.

We would contend that the model of empowerment dissected by Delgado-Gaitan and Trueba may well apply to other situations where social isolation promotes feelings of helplessness, passivity and fatalism. In this work, they specifically highlight how social isolation begins to be overcome as individuals come together to recognize in others their own predicament. Once this insight is gained, mobilization and commitment fuel the process of community involvement and input. Voices in the past such as that of Saul Alinsky, working in the 'behind the stockyards district' of Chicago in the 1940s, have tried to deliver the awakening message about the need for community action, and how to spread the word of how democratic empowerment works.

Whether in the educational, or occupational economic sphere, community action must be sustained from within to be effective. Trained outsiders cannot remain permanently. They can only instigate and stimulate. At best they are teachers, not permanent administrators. Social welfare, or any form of social amelioration of problems cannot be successfully administered alone by professional outsiders, even by a well meaning or relatively well trained bureaucracy. Social welfare is not democracy, public participation is. The school is part of a community and cannot be effective without public participation.

A central thrust of this work, which directly stems from participant observation over a number of months, is the nature of an inner sense of empowerment necessary to parents, and to the ethnic community generally for effective interaction with the school as an institution. Schools cannot work if there is no input from the community in the educative process. The authors realize that the essence of American democracy is this necessary interaction between the specialists trained for specific functions and the community being served.

It is not the task of the school, peopled by teachers drawn from the majority society, to 'acculturate' minorities to be part of a melting down process of assimilation. In a multiethnic society no one needs to be melted down, but they do need to be encouraged to participate in public processes. Public activity, however, is not limited to periodic voting, but includes continual input into the management of schools.

It is the role of the school to be an educative service to the community into which it has been placed. Contrary to many suppositions among the majority, our new minorities *are* vitally interested in the successful educational adaptation of their children. Indeed, immigrant minorities around the world want a better tomorrow. The dream immigrants pursue is also a better life for their children. And schooling, more often than not, emerges among immigrants as the key to a better tomorrow.

Immigrants often know full well that their children in the US have a precious opportunity to study and to better themselves, an opportunity the parents could not realize in their home countries.

The problem often is that immigrant minority parents have no sense of *how* to become involved, how to have concrete input, how to operationalize their dream. Nor is there sufficient or effective effort made to involve them. The middle class majority remains generally unmindful of how to overcome reluctance on the part of ethnic or working class parents who must discomfort themselves by entering into unfamiliar group processes wherein they feel lack of equal status.

This type of situation is what Concha Delgado-Gaitan and Henry Trueba are examining in their 'ethnography of empowerment'. Understanding how to instigate or implement the inner experience of empowerment, if and when it occurs, is a new key to the true democratization of the school in society. Anthropology has a role in understanding this process. Delgado-Gaitan and Trueba have made a notable contribution to such understanding in this volume.

George A. DeVos
University of California, Berkeley
Marcelo M. Suárez-Orozco
University of California, San Diego

Introduction

The United States is an amazing country because it embraces so many different ethnic groups, philosophical doctrines, diverse behavioral and belief systems, and a variety of lifestyles and social classes. America continues to attract individuals from all over the world to come and share in the dream of a good life in freedom and democracy. Indeed it is the search for this dream that effectively rekindles our democratic ideals with every wave of newcomers. The adventurous, and sometimes desperate, efforts of immigrants are the most precious investment ethnic communities make for their children. Because most members of the families in these ethnic groups have a profound sense of belonging together as a community, of sharing whatever they have, they work very hard to improve their lives and those of their community members. They feel they are truly opening new opportunities for the children in the community. Ethnic families are committed to helping their children succeed in America.

This book is about the way that the first generation of Hispano children are reared by immigrant parents in one community. The potential of human resources is evident in home, school and community socialization practices. The children's transition from novices in the US system to more experienced participants is not a linear path for immigrant families. It requires a drastic cultural and social change, the acquisition of new cultural knowledge, new language and new values and varies largely according to the family's socioeconomic, political, and educational opportunities. Often the transition represents a change from a rural home environment to an advanced technological society with complex norms of behavior and sophisticated communication systems. In order to adjust to a new technologically advanced society, immigrant and refugee families (especially children) must have high motivation and clear rewards. The process of adjustment is contingent on the motivation level and the preparation (social and cultural knowledge) possessed by the family and the institutional responsiveness to the needs of children and their families. Chapter One provides the reader with the background on culture, motivation and education for adjustment of ethnic and linguistic minority students. It presents in a crosscultural perspective the concept of culture in new learning environments members of ethnic communities must face when they come to this country in search of opportunities.

Formerly accepted authoritative statements by the federal government and other agencies attempting to explain the academic failure of language minority students in terms of their lack of English proficiency is now seriously questioned by theoreticians. In the first place, it ignores the sociohistorical determinants of minority students' school failure. Second, the question of what exactly constitutes proficiency in English is left vague, despite its central importance to the entire rationale (Cummins, 1989:21).

The oversimplification of the relationship between language and culture, and the fundamental ignorance of the role of culture in the acquisition of knowledge has led some researchers to serious misunderstandings of the ability of ethnic/linguistically different students. An example will illustrate this point. Dunn (1987), primary author of the Peabody Picture Vocabulary Test stated:

> While it is a very delicate and controversial topic, race, as a contributing factor, cannot be ignored. It is recalled from Part I of Dunn's (1987) monograph that most Hispanic immigrants to the US are brown-skinned people, a mix of American Indian and Spanish blood, while Puerto Ricans are dark-skinned, a mix of Spanish, black, and

some Indian. Black and American Indians have repeatedly scored about 15 IW points behind Anglos and Orientals on individual tests of intelligence ... (Dunn, 1987:64).

Reconstructing the flawed argument of genetic determination of intelligence, he ignores the socioeconomic and cultural differences of Spanish-speaking students and suggests that bilingual education could somehow contribute to the disintegration of the United States of America (1987:66–67) because Latino children — being mixed genetically — and adults are inferior and speak an inferior variety of the Spanish language in comparison with the children from the mainland. In a gesture of generosity and liberalism, Dunn closes his argument as follows:

Therefore, based on these factors my best tentative estimate is that about half of the IQ difference between Puerto Rican or Mexican American school children and Anglos is due to genes that influence scholastic aptitude, the other half to environment (Dunn, 1987:64).

Individuals like Dunn seem not only to ignore the nature of the relationship between language, culture and cognition, but the fundamental historical fact that many of the ethnic/linguistically different children have done fairly well despite the failure of schools to recognize their potential and despite the consistent pressure to make them sacrifice their ethnic identity, their language and culture, as a condition for acceptance in this society. The Secoya study brings refreshing data on how children integrate their home and school cultural values, and find ways to adjust and succeed in great measure because of the support of their parents and home/community environment. Some of these children, however, as early as the second grade face signs of serious disengagement with the schooling process. More problematic is the school's inattention to the nature of the situation as they deal with only the surface symptoms of children's behavior. The genetic determination of intelligence has been discredited for several decades and the arguments against it have been summarized by Cummins (1984) and all the authors of the special 1988 issue of the *Hispanic Journal of Behavioral Sciences* (see especially Trueba, 1988d:253–262).

This book disputes deficit arguments like the ones built by Dunn and it builds a profile of Hispano children at work in the home, school and community. Chapter Two provides a descriptive account of Secoya, its character, history, ethnic composition, population trends and its overall social and cultural features. This chapter provides the necessary context to understand what the daily experiences of the Hispano children really mean to them. The problems faced by immigrant and refugee children are created by social and cultural factors beyond the control of schools. In any attempts to launch school reform it is important to recognize the impact of the social and cultural environment outside of the school. This basic truth becomes even more clear in the study of youngsters' socialization across cultures. George and Louise Spindler remind us that:

... school, just as in the Arunta and Hutterite cases, and in thousands of other cultures, is borne, endured, survived, accomplished, because it is geared to success, not failure, and because success means a place, a productive, acceptable place in the social, economic and honorific scheme of things. There is an assured and assumed continuity, whatever the compressions, constraints, threats and anxiety aroused may be. The system is self-sustaining. The outcome assures the reduction of dissonance and identification with desired goals; and the cultural system has recruited new members committed to its maintenance (Spindler and Spindler, 1989:13).

What shapes the child's view of the social and cultural environment is the home socialization, that process of discovery of the world through the eyes of family members and others closely related to the child. Chapter Three of this volume walks the reader through the family life, values, norms and routines that prepare the child to face the outside reality of school, community and the world at large. A central issue in this chapter is the role of parents in assisting children to learn, to acquire basic knowledge and strategies leading to more effective schooling. Disciplinary practices, parents' commitment to make children succeed, overall family style and home culture are seen at a close range. The impact of school on children's home life is evident. The children's talent for integrating values, priorities and demands from home and school reveals their significant potential for accomplishing their goals in schools and life in general. This is the quintessence of the realization of the American dream, in the day-to-day sacrifice of one member of the family for the others, and in the collective commitment to succeed. The reality of American democracy that is being discovered and reconstructed every day by immigrant families is finally narrowed down to the enormous energy invested by parents supporting their children the best they can, in the midst of poverty, limited English language proficiency, and the overwhelming task of acquiring a new set of sociocultural values.

Storytelling and games, discussed in Chapter Four, show the reader the increasing ability of children to use the language, concept and strategies learned in school, while retaining their own particular lifestyle and values. The nature of the changes they make in their games and verbal exchanges and the creativity of their thinking as they interact manifests high cognitive flexibility and profound understanding of the importance of new cultural values, competition and academic knowledge.

The journey from home to school and back home never ends. As children repeat the cycle they are impacted by both home and school. Chapter Five specifically focuses on what values, knowledge and patterns of behavior they bring back home and with what consequences. Parents learn through their children what the world outside is like and how the challenge of cultural change must be faced. Reflections on the schools, parental expectations and their overall hopes and dreams are discussed. The authors felt privileged to have been a part of these families' world and to present to the reader some of the most salient views and insights held by those involved in the study. The following chapters describe the methodology used to get at an inside view of immigrant families and discuss the consequences of that view for educational reform.

Chapter Six attempts to build a statement on the nature of

ethnographic research designed to study a people's transition from either alienation or isolation, to one of full participation in social democratic institutions. The chapter describes the nature of power and the process of empowerment as a perspective and way of explaining cultural change in the Secoya community and broader surroundings. Defining an ethnography of empowerment as a distinct methodological and theoretical approach to the study of American democracy in the making is a complex task, but one worth raising even with initial modest theoretical statements. This chapter describes the social and cultural context in which an ethnography of empowerment develops, and the set of assumptions (philosophical, theoretical and methodological) with which educational anthropologists have developed the ethnography of empowerment. At a more formative stage is the role of ethnographic research as a tool to organize interventions intended to empower ethnic, linguistic, and low socioeconomic groups in a democratic society, and particularly in the United States. The role played by educational researchers has been changing from a seemingly 'objective' scientific position that ignores the construction of meaning by the research participants while imposing external explanations of the native experience to one of advocacy for the communities that open themselves up to be studied but remain structurally isolated. This change is particularly noticeable in the anthropological and sociological literature. Other important theoretical changes and advances are also recorded in this chapter.

Chapter Seven leads the reader to a discussion of the implications of an ethnography of empowerment for educational reform. This chapter suggests categories of information useful to understanding the social and cultural context of schools prior to designing any intervention: for example the ethnohistorical development of the community and school, the social climate around the school, the organization and management of the school, the characteristics of teachers and other school personnel, the organization of the curriculum and classroom instruction, and the response of students to instructional practices. The volume goes full cycle, from the children's home to the school and the social environment, from the social environment to the home and their impact each other. The process of acquiring this knowledge (ethnographic research) has the potential to drive reform strategies. Indeed an ethnography of empowerment can be highly instrumental in educational reform and in the making of American democracy.

Chapter 1

The Role of Culture in Learning

Culture defined as social shared cognitive codes and maps, norms of appropriate behavior, assumptions about values and world view, and lifestyle in general, profoundly influences the way we humans think and act. Ultimately, as Goodenough has stated, culture 'is made up of the concepts, beliefs, and principles of action and organization' (1976:5).

Culture exists in every context and plays a role in the way that people function. But cultures vary, from place to place and from time to time. Because our culture concept is so fundamental to our individual reality, we sometimes find it difficult to understand others' culture. The problem is not only observing and interpreting another's cultural behavior, but 'specifying under what conditions it is culturally appropriate to anticipate that he, or persons occupying his role, will render an equivalent performance' (Frake, 1964:112).

American culture seems extremely complex because it has incorporated populations with different cultures and varying social strata from all over the world. On the other hand, an important aspect of American culture has been to create uniformity, conformity and synchrony (Spindler and Spindler, 1990). The continued debate over what American culture is and how minorities participate in it is illuminated by the Spindlers' observations over the last thirty years. At the heart of their discussion is both the concept of cultural transmission from one generation to another, and the role schools play in the acculturation of minorities especially with regard to the values of American democracy and respect for cultural differences.

Anthropologists who have devoted their lives to the study of culture in a broad cross-cultural comparative perspective have also followed the flow of immigrant, minority and refugee populations around the world. These anthropologists have pointed out the differential response of such groups to educational settings in industrial societies (DeVos and Wagatsuma, 1966; DeVos, 1980, 1982, 1988; Ogbu, 1974, 1978, 1982, 1987). The problems arising from efforts to explain differential performance of minorities have been the focus of many recent studies (for summaries, see Trueba, 1988c, 1989).

These studies often attempt to answer the basic question confronted in this volume: What is the role of culture in achievement motivation and what is its influence on the actual learning abilities and academic performance of racial, ethnic, linguistic, refugee, low-income and other minority students? Research efforts geared to answer this fundamental question (and sets of related questions) have now built a solid cross-cultural theoretical base which is typically interdisciplinary within the social sciences. The questions have been more important than the answers, because they have led researchers to ask more appropriate questions and to redirect their studies. Current research is looking into 'learning environment' beyond micro-analysis of learning processes or learning activities. What follows is a presentation of some of the preliminary discussions on learning environments. The specific focus of the discussion in this chapter will be on cultural diversity and achievement in schools — schools seen as one of children's learning environments — and some interdisciplinary approaches to the study of diversity in schools as opposed to home learning environments.

Achievement Motivation in Cross-Cultural Settings

The transmission of cultural knowledge and values is at the foundation of problems related to the adjustment and academic achievement of ethnically and linguistically different students. Studies of the role of ethnicity and culture in achievement motivation have raised important theoretical and methodological questions regarding the need for interdisciplinary and cross-cultural approaches. For example, DeVos recently pointed out the following:

> In the United States, we have noted the differential response of various minority groups to educational adaptation within American society. On the one hand, some Asian groups are doing relatively well, having taken to the school system in a positive way; they are over-represented numerically according to population at many of the major undergraduate and graduate institutions of advanced learning. Other groups, such as the Mexican Americans and Blacks, have done relatively poorly in the American setting. Other instances of adaptation of ethnic minorities with particular histories of discrimination within a majority dominated school system are under examination. Research in reference to this question is just being initiated in a number of countries. For example, anthropologists and other social scientists in Belgium and Sweden are begining studies of the children of migrants in North European industrial states (1988:1).

The presence of ethnically and linguistically different populations in industrial societies is indeed an international phenomenon. The historical context of the previously quoted observations made by DeVos is crucial here. For example, Japan formally occupied Korea in 1910 and forced Koreans to engage in 'Japanization' programs with the purpose of increasing Japanese control over the colonized people. These programs were carried out through techniques and principles based on 'social attitudes of derogation and depreciation' discussed in detail by DeVos and his associates (DeVos, 1967, 1973, 1978, 1980, 1983, 1984, 1988; DeVos and Wagatsuma, 1966; Wagatsuma and DeVos, 1984). The programs of Japanization took the form of coercive governmental policies forcing Koreans to adopt Japanese language and lifestyle without full acceptance or equitable treatment; employment, residency standards and marriage laws were discriminatory. The oppressive relationship established by Japanese policies resulted in what DeVos and Ogbu have called the caste-like status of minorities. DeVos has discussed in detail the role of degradation incidents characteristic of coercive colonial policies (1984).

In studying the tragic recent history of South African violence — the Black majority oppressed under White minority forces in an anachronistic colonial system of exploitation — we have failed to focus on the consequences for the children of the oppressed in terms of their full intellectual development and their motivation to achieve. Similar situations occur in countries other than South Africa. DeVos (1988) and Suárez-Orozco (1989) have developed theories of minority adjustment, coping behaviors and achievement motivation. Their research methodology combines ethnohistorical and field-based ethnographic approaches with the use of projective techniques. The focus of their studies is on the role of the culture and cultural conflict in the complex transition of minority populations from the home country to industrial societies. Minority students face cultural conflicts that, under certain circumstances, may decrease their motivation to achieve as well as their actual performance. The central questions DeVos asks are the following:

1 Under what conditions can minority students maximize their achievement motivation and adapt to new learning environments?
2 Why does the same ethnic or minority population achieve more in one society than in another? (1988).

Culture and ethnicity are no longer concepts relegated to speculative and esoteric discussion in obscure corners of academia. Cultural, racial and ethnic identity concepts have come to life in the midst of violence, as well as national and international politics. These concepts must be debated and discussed as integral parts of a philosophy of life that affects the very existence of industrial societies, including ours. The realization that increasing numbers of immigrant and refugee workers from colonized, impoverished and desperate countries are emigrating to powerful industrial countries in increasing numbers has not arrived at its ultimate consequences. The labor force in industrial countries is more politicized, costly, and less efficient than that of poor underdeveloped countries. These people, fighting for survival, can vitalize a labor force in trouble. But immigrant and refugee workers are not coming alone, they bring children, wives, extended families, and more importantly, they bring their language and culture. With their motivation to build a more secure economic future for themselves and their families, they are willing to make a compromise between their cultural norms and those of the new land. That compromise is the basis for the conflict in which their children are born and raised. Often employers and teachers forget that the price of uprooting children from the home culture and planting them in a new culture can be very high in terms of achievement and overall psychological adjustment.

Cultural adjustment of immigrant and other minorities (especially the second and third generation of disenfranchised children of immigrants and refugees) is not an exclusive concern of the people in the United States. Suárez-Orozco, using DeVos' and Ogbu's theoretical frame has invoked the term 'castification' (meaning a process of marginalizations in the context of colonial oppression of minorities) applied to the children of immigrants and refugees in countries where there is systematic abuse of minorities. The alienation of ethnically and economically diverse populations is a serious concern of most industrial societies today, including Japan, Australia, New Zealand and certain Central and South American countries — Costa Rica, Brazil, Argentina, Chile — and especially European countries.

Neglect of immigrant, refugee and other minority children (low-income, uprooted and disenfranchised) constitutes an international crisis that is placing in jeopardy the future of democratic societies all over the world. In the middle of this crisis, while many children search for a home country with a clear sense of cultural values, hoping to belong somewhere, universities, schools of education and school districts become distracted with arguments over petty issues of jurisdiction and resources. When the house is burning, it does not make sense to quarrel over whose responsibility it is to supply the water! Why are the educational leaders of research institutions conspicuously absent from planning groups involving minority education? Is it because educational leaders come from a rather narrow theoretical framework acquired in their somewhat isolated university environment? Is it that they cannot grasp the significance and proportions of the problems associated with ethnicity and education? Or is it that linguistic and cultural differences, home culture and traditions, and low achievement of minority youngsters are all taken lightly as signs of trivial or passing phenomena that will eventually disappear in the melting pot of modern technological societies? Do educational leaders realize that melting pots do not 'melt' ethnically diverse individuals (although they may sometimes fry them into 'burnouts'). The 'melting pot' concept of minority acculturation becomes a veiled attack against cultural pluralism. In fact, we know that many ethnically linguistically different children are forced to jump out of the melting pot in their search for survival. Does the anger of these children, turned inward against themselves or outward against society in a rejection of their home culture worry modern educational leaders?

This book is intended to raise issues about minority children in the process of transition from their home culture to that of the school. The authors argue that issues of cultural and linguistic differences in large ethnic and minority populations have important and lasting consequences affecting the very fabric of democratic societies, and that they require study and understanding. The price of negligence or oversimplification appears to be high enough that certain European countries are now investing heavily in creating research and policy centers composed of anthropologists, sociologists, psychologists, demographers, linguists and educators.

This first chapter attempts to articulate the important concept of cultures in learning environments and ethnic communities in interaction with mainstream cultures. These concepts will be discussed in the context of the rapid increase of ethnic, linguistic and economic minority students in industrial societies, especially the United States. These concepts become interrelated in the process of socialization and acculturation. The socialization of uprooted children (children from racial, linguistic, ethnic, refugee, or low-income minority background) is characterized by common responses to cultural conflict and to demands for rapid acculturation. These demands take the form of pressure for a speedy and successful adjustment to a new lifestyle, effective use of a new language, and clear commitment to a new set of cultural values. Tolerance for different paces in acculturation or language acquisition is low. A deeper understanding of the nature of the transition from home to school is often missing. Consequently, specifically relevant to this volume is the discussion of the relationship between home and school socialization, the influence of home in school, and the impact of school in the homes of minority students. While the general purpose of this volume is to gain an insight into the process of socialization of minority children, the authors also suggest some theoretical advances in the study of the unique learning environments in which minority children find themselves.

Teachers and the Teaching of Culturally Diverse Students

The study of learning environments and the role that culture plays in them has attracted recent attention on the part of educational anthropologists. School learning environments have come under closer scrutiny. The teacher's role has been conceptualized as that of a bricoleur (in the sense used by Levi-Strauss, 1966:19–22). As Hatton explains: 'Bricoleurs on the technical plane develop and add to their repertoires of means through experience, hazard, luck, and imagination. They do not add to them in a principled, theoretically motivated fashion' (1989:80).

On the purely pragmatic plane, teachers tend to function at a rather rudimentary level. Pressed by competing demands for their attention, teachers have no time to develop a theory of teaching effectiveness:

> Their intellectual bricolate will involve ordering, explaining ... within the confines of a limited, fixed, unquestioned framework. Moreover, the explanatory categories to which they will appeal will be those provided by sensory perception and almost certainly those of crude psychology. The explanations that teachers give of phenomena they encounter in school sometimes resemble the appearance of explanation within prior science. For

example, some teachers are inclined to explain comparative lack of academic achievement in working-class schools in terms of extraordinarily unsophisticated deficit theories (Hatton, 1989:80).

Teachers are faced with a relative inability to understand the nature, causes and consequences of cultural conflicts in minority populations. In order to see the profound historical relationships between social stratification and the causes of lower academic performance exhibited by minority students, they would need intensive study of the social and cultural contexts of instruction with its multiple aspects of communication, transfer of knowledge, transfer of cultural values, selective socialization and network of relationships.

The discussion of culture seems to have special significance for instructors only in instances where conflict brings a contrast of students' responses, or the responses of ethnic community members. Unexpected responses (in the form of kinetic or linguistic behaviors) in the same instructional settings attract teachers' attention and invite reflection. If Chinese students spend all night at the university computer laboratory more often than mainstream students or members of other ethnic groups, the instructors develop a theory of Chinese behavior: 'Chinese are culturally determined to pursue difficult tasks without appropriate rest and under difficult circumstances.' Or if Mexican American students more often than others fall sleep in early morning classes instructors may make the following inference: 'Mexican American students have no ambition; they are uninterested in the subject; they do not understand the subject and get bored.' The first hypothesis about the Chinese might be in the right direction, but the latter may lack evidence and ignore certain facts. For example, the Mexican American students may work two jobs to support a family, or they may have to travel a great distance. Instructors tend to make inferences to guide their assessment of a student's ability and performance and to formulate operating policies accordingly. Chinese students are seen as ambitious and hard-working, Mexican Americans as lazy. These attributes are linked to cultural values and part of the socialization process at home.

Culture, as an overall view of life that influences collective behavior, life style, value priorities, actions and thinking patterns, is not equally shared by the members of any society, not even by the members of the same social class or ethnic group in a single society. Each person's micro-sociological unit (community, family, peer group, church organization, voluntary association) plays an important role in creating specific sets of experiences shared collectively by individuals of those units, but interpreted by each in a different way. Ultimately, individuals select, under the influence of adults, the path of socialization which determines the meaning of their experiences. The differential control exercised by individuals over their experiences, in contrast to the control collectivities have over the life of individuals (for example, the power of social groups in determining norms of behavior in different social strata) constitutes a significant characteristic of culturally-determined socialization processes. This control vested in the individual has also implications for the mechanism chosen by immigrants to adjust to new cultures, modern industrial and technological societies.

The human species is characterized by the creation of language, a unique symbolic system for the transmission of knowledge and values from generation to generation. Language is a unique symbolic system because it helps to define, interpret, classify, store or communicate mental messages. Language, as the instrument *par excellence* for social intercourse, is essential in establishing the parameters of membership in social groupings and in opening the lines of communication. Not only through its spoken and written forms, but through kinetic, paralinguistic and other forms of face-to-face communications, language ultimately establishes social relationships and ongoing meaningful exchanges.

We can speculate that the early humans used language to transfer important messages related to group cohesiveness (differential roles within the early family or kin groups) as well as strategies for survival in the face of common dangers from more powerful mammals and from natural phenomena. As human groups began to differentiate and grow in population size, they developed more elaborate systems of communication and unique forms of conducting human activities related to basic human

survival: eating, mating, and protecting each other. The transmission of human knowledge has increased rapidly in a
relatively short time producing very complex and different patterns of thought and behavior among diverse cultural groups.
Knowledge is packed in linguistically and culturally meaningful
units that distinguish one group of individuals from another.
Unique histories, languages and cultures distinguish groups of
people who pursue their own cultural goals and overarching
values. Technical knowledge and the pursuit of technological
developments has become a top priority for Western societies.
In contrast, the oral transmission of folklore, traditional culti-
vation patterns (such as slash-and-burn agriculture) and the
maintenance of life without disturbing the ecological balance in
mountains or tropical forests, have been at the core of preindustrial societies. The value of literacy and language development in
industrial societies is pivotal to its cultural values and maintenance. As a consequence, the socialization of preindustrial
peoples in the United States requires a drastic change in cultural
values and an intense process of language and literacy acquisition
to meet the demands of our technological society.

Stratification and Language Change

In the United States, linguistic and social practices of ethnic and
linguistically different groups often differ considerably from the
mainstream values and behaviors that are usually expected in
the schools. Although sociocultural changes occur naturally
within cultural groups, antagonistic conditions determined by
social institutions such as schools force minority children to
abandon their native values and adopt mainstream norms. Mead
(1943) criticized modern education for creating cultural alienation: 'Changing people's habits, people's ideas, people's language, people's beliefs, people's emotional allegiances, involved
a sort of deliberate violence to other people's developed persona-
lities' (1943:637). Spoken like a true anthropologist, Mead
objected to changing people's culture as a way of rejecting the
popular notion in the United States that people of different
cultural identity should become assimilated in order to function

in this society. Faced with this adversity, immigrant group children have major adjustments to make when they go to school.

Children's home, play and classroom interactions are interrelated. Language change for children is influenced by their outside community. Thus if a community is largely Spanish-speaking, children's English language learning will inevitably be different from that of Spanish-speaking children in a predominantly English-speaking community (Fishman, 1976; McLaughlin, 1985). This book presents the relationship among interactions in these contexts with a focus on the role of children's activities in their social environment. The concept of sociocultural, linguistic and social interaction codes provides understanding to children's patterns of negotiation between the home and school cultures.

Appropriate sociocultural behavior within a group of people generally means that they are approved and rewarded by the adult members of the community. The cultural group, including families and friends, promotes desired behaviors through modeling and verbal and non-verbal communication. These patterns of interaction are learned and practiced in several socioeconomic environments, such as the home, school and the community at large. The type of language and social norms acquired by children are largely determined by a variety of complex factors. For example, where the families reside, where the adults are employed, where families go for recreation, religious and educational services greatly influence how children respond to learning language. For children of linguistic minority groups, language acquisition becomes even more complex, as they often interact in multiple language groups and must therefore acquire new norms of interaction.

Educators often assume that children's low achievement is explained by their lack of the English language communication etiquette expected in school (Trueba, 1989; Trueba, 1990). However, this assumption fails to recognize the native skills of Spanish-speaking children. To state that all sociocultural conflict results in underachievement implies that Spanish speaking home socialization does not prepare children sufficiently for school. However, desirable and expected adaptation can be observed in limited-English-speaking children learning in a new cultural setting (Diaz, Moll and Mehan, 1986). The very act of learning English as a second language is a cultural variation, but it does not necessarily create distress for children. A conflict ensues when children limited in English proficiency are taught all their academic curriculum in English in such a way that their native language and culture are invalidated. Although English is necessary to the children's successful and meaningful participation in the classroom and in society, the language must be taught appropriately, in the context of real experience (Goodman, 1986; Krashen and Terrell, 1983). Learning English, on the other hand, does not preclude students from developing and maintaining their native language, especially in bilingual classrooms (Cummins, 1981, 1986; Hakuta, 1986).

The Secoya study reported here suggests that the issue of sociocultural changes in language and other social norms is neither positive or negative. That is, whether or not Spanish-speaking children learn English and acculturate into mainstream values cannot be seen as good or bad unless we understand the social context in which those phenomena occur. It is only in the social context that we learn about the knowledge of those in interaction with each other and their goals for what they want to accomplish. It also follows that if we argue that cultural compatibility between the home and the school is not necessarily desirable in the formal teaching setting, then we also have to state that not all cultural incompatibilities are undesirable, even though they must be accommodated appropriately in the school. Changes in social or cultural patterns exist as a natural consequence of cultural contact. While some points of conflict occur, it is incorrect to assume all sociocultural changes are negative. The question, then, remains: why is language change for Spanish-speaking Hispanic children such a critical research issue? The answer to this quest lies not only in the classroom but in school contexts.

Sociologists and sociolinguists are aware of the importance of social stratification and its endurance across generations to the point of creating a quasi-caste system in industrial societies. Some models of status attainment use components such as socioeconomic status of individuals (parents' educational background and occupation and language proficiency). Mehan offers the following insight:

> Casting the issue of social stratification in this succinct form [in terms of socioeconomic background and personal achievement] is extremely useful because it helps us conceptualize the relative influence of background variables and schooling on attained status. Some theories view schooling as a channel of social mobility; others view schooling as a transmitter of status advantages from generation to the next ... (1984:174).

If indeed stratification and social status are important in industrial societies, and if language acquisition (English as a second language) is the appropriate mechanism for achieving upward social mobility by linguistically different groups, then the relationship of language, schooling and stratification deserves serious attention from social scientists and educational researchers. On these issues, anthropologists, sociolinguists and sociologists have generated important research in the last two decades (see Gumperz and Hymes, 1964, 1972; Philips, 1983; Gilmore and Glatthorn, 1982; Heath, 1983; Cook-Gumperz, 1986; Gumperz, 1986; Erickson, 1984; Hernandez-Chavez, 1984; Cummins, 1984, 1986, 1989; Rueda, 1987; Hornberger, 1988; Trueba and Delgado-Gaitan, 1988; Trueba, 1989; Trueba, Spindler and Spindler, 1990; Trueba, Jacobs and Kirton, 1990; and many others).

Older generations of social scientists and educational researchers, however, did not expect to have in the same town, much less in the same school (and even in the same classroom) children from many diverse cultures and social strata — from industrial societies and from preindustrial societies, from Western and Eastern countries, from contemporary European technologically developed countries, and from the most isolated peasant societies. What was surprising both in Europe and the United States was not so much the unusual presence of diverse ethnic and social groups with diametrically opposed cultural value systems, but the rapid changes that these groups are experiencing in the United States and European countries. In the Central

Valley of California, for example, which has about seventy different linguistic groups, the Hmong refugee population increased from approximately 5,000 to 26,000 between 1980 and 1989. By October 1989 the state of California has attracted about 45,000 out of the 96,000 Hmong refugees in the country. In Sacramento, California, between 1988 and 1989, several schools increased their ethnic minority student population by about 30 per cent due primarily to the arrival of additional refugee and immigrant families. Several schools in West Sacramento opened in the fall of 1989 with a refugee and immigrant student population of 70 per cent (up from 35 per cent from the previous year). Some children arrived in the US three weeks before the Fall term started.

In the United States there are close to 40,000,000 speakers of over 120 major languages other than English. California has the unique distinction of having become the first state in the union whose ethnic, linguistic and racial 'minority' populations constituted over 50 per cent of the entire state population. Most modern industrial societies sharing a common democratic structure and economic needs due to labor shortages opened the door to immigrant and refugee populations (preferably on a temporary basis). They hire willing hands, but with the hands come bodies, and wives and children and extended families, and new languages and cultures vastly different from the host society. A short-term economic investment in cheap labor becomes a long term cultural investment in cultural pluralism, a pluralism (at least initially) perceived as congruent with our democratic form of government and our philosophy.

Today cultural diversity is manifested in the brutal reality of Monday morning in a San Francisco downtown street where children waiting in line for the school bus observe the drunkards and prostitutes, the homeless and mentally ill, the drug addicts and the dope pushers: close range contact with disenfranchised Americans. Cultural diversity is the hard reality of a first grade class in central California where there are so few English-speaking children that the teacher can find no one to match her Non English-speaking Proficient (or NEP) children, no one to answer a simple question about colors or days of the week. Collectively, the children speak seven or eight different languages other than English, but the teacher knows none of those languages.

As ethnic children attend school and begin to speak some English, their comprehension of the relationship between their home culture and the school culture (indeed the culture of the larger society) becomes more elusive and confusing. At times children are torn between competing linguistic and cultural codes, or worse still between conflicting sets of cultural values and life styles. Still more difficult is the task of defining their own self-concepts in a meaningful way. Here is where the cultural and social conflicts between home and school can become a nightmare of contrasting demands that confuse or lead to rejection of the home culture and language, and even in some extreme cases to rejection of one's own self.

Self rejection, and the overall rejection of the home culture precludes children from using the home learning environment to develop their full potential. This rejection often creates a deep emotional schism between the child and the family, and can place undue stress on the child to seek appropriate behaviors from a limited repertoire of cultural experiences; these conflicts ultimately result in emotional or learning handicaps. The complex characteristics of the home culture, not as a static set of values and relationships, but as a rapidly changing world of ideas, is seen in the impact that schools have in the ethnic homes. If the schools ignore the significance of the home learning environment there is a serious loss for the child and for the school. Parents of ethnic and linguistically different children can become a strong support for academic learning, and can help smooth the transition of children from one cultural environment to another. Pressure on children to relinquish their language and culture carries a high price. Some children never recover from the trauma of losing the mother tongue before they can acquire a new language; they often become 'learning disabled'.

Other children may achieve normally in school, but become socially and psychologically unable to work with others in the society. They are unable to integrate the values of the home culture with those of their new culture. Eventually, they turn against the new culture and reject it too. For example, the profound anger shown by some ethnic and minority youths against persons representing 'mainstream American' culture is translated into anti-social behavior against authority, legal and educational institutions, public property, or even against democratic principles in general.

There is a great deal of public sensitivity with regard to the development of marginal cultural groups in America, such as the homeless, the hippies, the drug-addicts, low-income, and other disenfranchised populations. There is some apprehension about diversity in the society and (even in the absence of hard data) there is a strong belief that people of ethnic and linguistically different groups represent a serious sociocultural, political and economic burden. Many mainstream persons do not acknowledge the sincere commitment of immigrant, ethnic, racial, refugee and other minority populations to become good citizens and to work hard in the pursuit of the American dream (Spindler and Spindler, 1990).

The Dilemma of Ethnic Identity

Learning varies for children depending on their social and cultural groups. Research has shown that learning is socioculturally bound and further compounded by gender, socioeconomic and language differences (Grant and Sleeter, 1986; Ortiz, 1988; Rumberger, 1989). Therefore, we need to examine learning acquisition not only in different populations but also within different settings in which children of the respective groups participate.

According to the US Bureau of the Census (1988) Hispanics represent about 10 per cent of the total population in the United States, but will comprise 25 per cent by the year 2000. Mexican Americans comprise about 20,000,000 which is about 63 per cent of the Hispanic population in the United States. In California alone, Mexican Americans number about 6,000,000 in 1990. Of the 7,500,000 school age children in California, children of Mexican American descent comprise 35 per cent (Evans, Wald, Smrekar, and Ventresca, 1989:13).

These statistics, in and of themselves, are insignificant except for the fact that about 45 per cent of the Mexican American students who enter high school drop out before they reach the tenth grade (Cortes, 1986). In some school districts across the country the percentage of Mexican American student dropouts has exceeded 52 per cent (Rumberger, 1989). This drop-out rate does not mean that Mexican Americans are not capable of learning. Many students who drop out of school are said to be intelligent students whom the school failed to provide with contexts that create learning (McDermott, 1977, 1987a, 1987b).

Intelligence, opportunity and access form the interdependent triangle of factors contributing to learning (De Avila, 1986). De Avila defines intelligence as that which a person does with what s/he has. In reference to Mexican American children, De Avila's research concludes that they are indeed intelligent but the educational problems they confront are exacerbated by the type of opportunities available and their access to those opportunities. Children have the opportunity to learn in school because the law provides that opportunity. For many, however, their access to learning opportunities is constrained by classroom or school policies and procedures that forbid them to use their home language to learn or that limit peer involvement in the classroom (Trueba, 1987, 1988b).

The failure to provide contexts by which children can learn in school have contributed to the complex factors that have caused Mexican American students to drop out of school in later years. Compounding factors include the students' personal self-identity aspirations and perceptions, family background, academic programs, and community support (Delgado-Gaitan, 1988a, 1988b; Fernandez, Paulsen, and Hirano-Nakanishi, 1989; Rumberger, 1989; Trueba, 1989). Most of the studies cited here have noted that while students tend to leave school in the early high school years, the process of dropping out begins much earlier. Students participate in their family, school, and community; how young students learn in these different settings must be examined to shed light on the process of knowledge acquisition in the early years.

The study of sociocultural competencies in knowledge acquisition in social contexts can take many directions. The social context of learning provides a lens into the personal relationships that shape children's language and values. In this book, we have chosen to describe and analyze children's interactions with adults and peers in their home tasks, play events, and classroom lessons because it made sense to present evidence on how a new generation of Mexican American children are reared by immigrant parents from Mexico whose experience in the United States is limited. This cohort comes close to comprising the majority group in California's schools. How does the home and community social and political ecology of these families affect the children's lives? What resources and networks do families share in their community as they attempt to socialize their children in a society that is vastly different from the experience which is familiar to them? Of greater consequence to educators, how does the school deal with these children when they go to school? These questions become important because those involved with education must understand the cultural changes experienced by children who widely populate their schools in an effort to better inform policy and practice.

Life experiences of Mexican families in the US spread on a broad continuum between Anglo-like competitive achievement and the more typical quiet, inconspicuous performance of other immigrant groups. Some children have been raised in the cultural tradition of cooperative work; therefore, they have a difficult time assuming competitive attitudes. Hesitancy to engage in competitive behavior eventually gives way to a sort of cultural code-switching from cooperation to competition.

One may see in one and the same day a Mexican American professional acting as a key person in a mainstream organization in the morning (a top executive, lawyer, teacher, or highly-skilled worker); then meeting at noon with other Hispanic colleagues; going home for supper in the evening; and finally attending a night community meeting in the barrio. This Mexican American could probably code-switch into five different linguistic/cultural interaction styles extending from formal, standard, mainstream English in the role of institutional representative to colloquial English and Spanish, used interchangeably without conspicuously excluding Anglo friends, to a formal Spanish in the home (with all the peculiar cultural and linguistic usages), to, finally, a barrio-type of Spanish (rural and mixed with 'Calo').

Professional Mexican Americans, for example, may seem to be as 'cut-throat' competitive as their Anglo counterparts, yet they develop inconspicuously collaborative working relationships with other Mexican American professionals — *inconspicuous* in order to avoid suspicion of being partial to other ethnics, and consequently unfit for business. They strive to meet the demands of the business world, while at the same time fulfilling their Mexican cultural goals of cooperation and reciprocity. This mode of competition is also uniquely Mexican. For example, it is not culturally appropriate in the Mexican traditional behavior patterns of most middle- or low-income immigrants to show overt aggression, or to express freely in public one's own personal feelings of pain, anger, jealousy, or love.

As Mexican Americans internalize mainstream cultural values, there is an increased expectation for them to express personal feelings freely and in public. However, this freedom is contextually appropriate only in the presence of other peers equally acculturated or of Anglo-American persons, not with older Mexicans who may interpret such expressions as lack of control and *mala educación* (bad manners). *Buena educación* or good manners consist of knowing one's own cultural values in fostering or preventing personal relationships, and remaining loyal to these relationships. Good manners emphasize generous hospitality interpreted as the offering of food, shelter and services to others without expectation of predictable or personal reciprocity. Parents continue to occupy a place of highest respect and authority even for grown-up children who live independently. Networking is primarily based on kinship of familial ties and has the purpose of providing emotional, social and economic support. There is a certain amount of distrust of the impersonal character of representatives of public institutions; thus, Mexican people often seek institutions in which they can develop personal relationships and rely upon them.

Religious beliefs remain strong in the Mexican family, especially in the context of life crisis situations (births, baptisms, confirmations, marriage, and death) or festivities occurring in the predictable liturgical calendar. It is assumed that religious beliefs will be acquired during the early years of socialization. Women (mothers and sisters especially) play a major role in the religious socialization of all children. Women's role and influence is defined in the context of the family. Professional women are less the norm in the labor force although their numbers are increasing rapidly on both sides of the border.

Males are the primary or only wage earners. Their status as economic supporters and their control of the finances is enhanced by the role of ultimate authority ascribed to them by Mexican culture. The mother, however, is often the one that controls most of the activities of the house, and the one that deals with school problems and decisions affecting the life and education of children. Conspicuous display of wealth, or consumption of expensive merchandise is discouraged. The rich often hide their wealth. People keep a respectful distance from friends who become rich. The more money you have the more responsible you become to help others, particularly the members of your extended family.

Cultural socialization within the family inculcates a certain amount of guilt and anxiety about using wealth conspicuously when members of the extended family are poor or close friends are poor. It becomes a matter of loyalty to *La Familia* (the extended family) and to *La Raza* (the whole community) to be discreet and humble. Insensitivity to other Mexicans, lack of hospitality, lack of respect to the elderly, taking sides against La Raza (seen as betraying your own people and siding with the *Gringos,*), or embarrassing your own parents, are examples of behaviors considered the most despicable, rendering perpetrators liable to be cut from social communication. These behaviors ultimately demonstrate disloyalty to La Raza.

Culture change and uprooting oneself from one's own country can be traumatic. It is a well-known phenomenon on both sides of the border that many Mexicans who lived in the United States for a long time (called in Mexico *Pochos*, a derogative term alluding to their accent or misuse of the Spanish language) feel rejected both in Mexico and in the United States. They travel periodically between the two countries searching for an identity they have lost, unaware of their unusual ability to function effectively both sides of the border. They feel equally out of place in both countries when they lose the mastery of the Spanish language (the language they learned as children) without ever being able to obtain full command of the English language. Mexican immigrants who arrive in this country in their middle age and who were isolated in rural areas tend to fall into this category of 'Pochos' and 'unstable transitionals.' They can become insecure and vulnerable, often attributing to racial prejudice behaviors which characterize bureaucracies all over the world. Some even make desperate attempts to 'pass for' mainstream Americans while they lose their ethnic identity and cultural heritage. These individuals are also characterized by their social and psychological isolation, and the conviction that the home language and culture are to blame for all their problems.

Some Mexican families take much longer than others to overcome the trauma of cultural transition during the process of 'forced assimilation' into American society. Many immigrants and their children continue to show serious psychological scars and a deep-seated resentment as a result of the prejudice they faced and the unacceptability of their differences by mainstream society. Richard Rodriguez' *Hunger of Memory* (1982) is one of the best examples of the effects that years of forced assimilation can produce and the misconception of some Mexican Americans who view their home language and culture as a barrier to success. Pressure to assimilate without access to the mainstream culture is bound to create internal conflict in children's development. Parents will neglect to socialize Mexican children in their own language and culture. Teachers will also fail to recognize the value of the home language and culture. The price of neglecting children's language and culture as the proper means to teach academic content in schools is a very high one, if we consider the long-term consequences of academic disenfranchisement and dropout phenomena.

Summary

This chapter has emphasized the interrelationships of culture, language and learning, and the need to study learning processes in specific learning environments. The successful adjustment of immigrant and refugee and other ethnically/linguistically different children is deeply related to the quality of the learning environments in which they grow, both at home and in school. Those environments which neglect children or expose them to traumatic experiences tend to cause children's self rejection and delay the development of learning motivation and learning skills. Teachers who are faced with a demanding job, often without the necessary training and guidance, seem to function as the 'bricoleurs' discussed by Hatton (1989), that is, as individuals with limited repertoires working under pressure and without necessary resources, always improvising, never able to develop the critical thinking skills and theoretical models that would permit them to understand learning principle in depth. Teachers who remain 'bricoleurs' cannot understand the historical and sociological reasons for minority children's level of academic performance, the role of culture, or the nature of the cultural conflicts taking place in the classroom. Linguistic and cultural differences are seen superficially as obstacles to concept development, rather than as resources or bridges to facilitate children's transition from their home culture and language to the language and culture of the school.

Given the enormous numbers of ethnically diverse children in modern industrial countries who come with languages and cultures varying from those of the host countries, the responsibility of policy makers and planners for the government is to develop interdisciplinary teams of researchers and practitioners to examine the educational problems of schools with high concentrations of ethnic and linguistic children. In the United States we now have states with a larger proportion of ethnically different populations than of the white persons. There are many schools in the Southwestern US with concentrations between 75 and 80 per cent (if not higher) of minority students. Examining the long-term effects of rejecting the home language and culture, the marginalization of ethnically/linguistically diverse students, and the processes of transition from the home culture to the larger culture of American institutions are essential in the planning of future technological and economic development, and the future of democratic institutions in the United States and internationally.

Chapter 2

The Sociocultural Environment in Secoya

Historically, Secoya dates back to the mid-nineteenth century. Much of the population at that time were Mexicans who had worked on the development of the railroad which arrived at Secoya in 1863 (Davey and Davey, 1988). The railroad connected Secoya to the adjacent communities, making travel easier, especially during the winter. The first train station still stands in the original location although it has undergone substantial renovation. Initially, the railroad was used for transporting agricultural products, although the shipping of lumber became the cornerstone of the transportation market.

Secoya was incorporated in 1867. This made it possible for the town to make necessary repairs of roads, bridges, and water systems. Lumber shipping was the biggest business in Secoya. But by the turn of the century, the redwood forest had dwindled, and the lumber business moved farther south. Other businesses surfaced to take its place, among these tanning, brewing, canneries and the flower industry.

In the early 19th century following the Spanish Mission days in California and the development of the railroad, the presence of the Mexicans in Secoya grew gradually until the post World War II period when it increased in major proportions. The national *bracero* program made it possible for many Mexican men to immigrate to the US as agricultural laborers. Aguilillans from Michoacan were well represented in migratory agricultural labor force. In their own homeland agriculture was the primary form of employment, making them valuable labor for the US agricultural market. Once they began working in the US many men chose to remain permanently. They were able to do so legally by obtaining contracts with employers in industries other than agriculture. This permission allowed them to travel between Mexico and the US. As laborers moved from the agricultural industry to other types of employment such as construction, they began to populate the more urban areas. New immigration laws in 1964 restricted immigration from Mexico but that did not limit the international migration between Secoya and Aguililla (Rouse, 1989). Families crossed the border from Aguililla to Secoya and from the Secoya to Aguililla. The transnational circuit has served to maintain ties between families on both sides of the border and transformed the class composition in the process while considering the family and the Aguililla community the fundamental obligation. By 1980 Aguilillans comprised several thousand and many stores and restaurants catered to their preferences.

Rouse's dissertation (1989) is a seminal work in discussing the historical development of the Mexican community in Secoya. His study about the Mexican migration relations between Aguililla and Secoya (our pseudonym in this study) extends beyond the demographic and structural description to explain how migration affects the family. His study reveals the external and internal impediments that are a source of constant tension for families as they make their decisions to stay in the US and maintain family unity with those in Mexico. While the plans of many Mexicans who immigrate to Secoya is to return to Aguililla, the actualization of their goal is often plagued with conflict. People work many long hours for little money in the US with hopes of returning to Aguililla and establishing their own farming operation but soon realize that their savings are inadequate to fulfill their dream (Rouse, 1989:196). In spite of the many sacrifices made by immigrant families as they attempt to expand their socioeconomic base in the US, there is no guarantee that they will have a more privileged position when they return to Mexico. During their stay in the US, immigrant families also face family struggles to maintain their cultural values and commitment on the face of sociopolitical and socioeconomic press in the US.

Accommodating Diversity in the Community

Secoya was selected as the research site for our study because of its large Spanish-speaking community that had managed to maintain their culture through constant immigration from Mexico. The community is similar to other urban immigrant areas like East Los Angeles where Spanish is represented in the local businesses and services, but differs from other Mexican immigrant-impacted communities like Portillo where most of the businesses do not reflect the people's language or culture (Delgado-Gaitan, 1990). The families in the study participated in extended social networks including religious, political and educational groups.

The east side of Secoya is an unincorporated geographic community in a Bay Area county which is a major metropolitan center on the west coast of the United States. The west side of Secoya is occupied by a more middle- to upper-class Anglo group of people than the section east of the main boulevard in town. Industrial activity is absent on the west side but thrives on the east section of town. Tool and die shops, chemical engineering corporations and lumber yards are in abundance. The east side of town is populated largely by Spanish-speaking people.

The groups identified within the Secoya Spanish speaking community include, Chicano, Mexican American and Mexican, Latino American and Central Americans. Of these people the population of Mexican descent comprises the largest group. They differ in four general ways: immigration patterns, language preference, traditional social practices, and employment. Although the participants in the study were legal immigrant Mexican and Central American families, the intent here is not to label people by indicating their ethnic identity, but rather to put into perspective the heterogeneity of the Spanish-speaking community in Secoya.

On the east side of Secoya, a variety of businesses line the main street of the community. These include medical services, local mechanics, numerous Mexican restaurants, grocery stores and butcher shops catering to the Mexican group, and a community center. In most of the businesses, store clerks, mechanics and waitresses speak Spanish. In 1989, the local newspaper ran an article referring to Secoya as 'Little Mexico', recognizing the strong presence of Mexicans in the community. Mexican Americans own local restaurants, produce markets, bakeries, and beauty shops while other businesses like landscape services, furniture and appliance stores are owned by Whites.

Various services are provided through the Secoya Community Center. These include translating services for filling out forms and correspondence, English classes for adults, legal immigration information and referrals for employment. Additionally, the Center provides a school nutrition project and a preschool program funded by the state. Although the preschool has an enrollment of 98 per cent Spanish-speaking children, a bilingual program has not been organized. Any Spanish language used in the preschool was used informally by the bilingual teacher assistants. The preschool program caters to working class families who can only afford a sliding-scale fee. The range of ages of the children is 3 to 4 years. Adjacent to the preschool project is a one-room bilingual branch of the city public library, recognizing the language diversity in the neighborhood. Great care is taken by the librarian to order children's books that reflect the ethnic and language composition of the community. Children of all ages frequent the library after school, and during the summer they attend the summer reading programs and use the library as a place to 'hang out'. Puzzles and other manipulative materials are made available to children throughout the year, and films, books, and free lunches attract many children to use the library as a place to socialize while their parents work. A lunch program is offered for adults during the summer months in a large dining room next to the library.

The Secoya Community Center is the pivotal point for youth social projects. Attempts have been made to employ *cholos* in constructive tasks such as writing a newsletter for the Center. One resident expressed the view that, because of the high drop-out rate among Chicano youths, it was important to integrate them into specific programs that could serve as preventive measures against delinquent activity in the neighborhood.

Political activity in the Secoya community Center is carried out through long-standing organizations. For example, the Civil Hidalgo Organization advocated the establishment of the

Victoria School Park, which received approval from the County Supervisors. Another organization serves as an advocate for people's rights in the workplace. The organization also advises renters of their right to live in affordable housing. Advocacy for the Spanish-speaking community seems to be the primary intent of the organizations. The Center is used as a meeting place although many organizations are not officially affiliated with it.

Well-groomed single-family dwellings are the most common housing structures in the neighborhood. Usually a small yard is attached either to the front or back, where children can be seen and heard as they play. The school playground is the nearest public recreation area for these residents and children, and adults often visit there after school hours and on weekends. Local soccer teams play on school playgrounds on weekends. The entire setting encompasses about a ten-block area. Two railroad tracks run through Secoya. One track separates low-income houses from more middle-income homes while the other track separates the low-income residential area from the more industrial part of Secoya.

At least 75 per cent of the Secoya residents are of Hispanic origin. Other visible ethnic groups include Blacks and Southeast Asian refugee groups. Oakgrove and Gardner Schools report that children of Mexican American backgrounds are between 80–85 per cent of their enrollment.

Merging Ethnic Borders

In Secoya, people seemed to have a compelling need to be identified for their specific values and practices inclusive of their ethnic group: Mexican, Mexican American, Salvadorian, Chileno or Puerto Rican. However, they perceived the ethnic unit of 'Hispano' as an essential common denominator necessary for political power.

The heterogeneity in 'Hispano' (a term adopted by people of Latino origin) communities reflects the protean character of the population, encompassing those of Mexican descent and others from Central America, Latino America, and, in Secoya, a small group from Puerto Rico. Members of Mexican descent are further split into ethnic identities — Chicano, Mexican American and Mexican — which seem to depend on their perceptions of each other. Although some were clearly Spanish-speaking and identified as Mexican when they first immigrated, they began to acquire a new identity as others perceived them as being more mainstream. More traditional Mexicans describe this group as Spanish-speakers who have not maintained the language, and who have adapted to the Anglo ways of life, particularly in the political arena. Identified as 'Hispano', the adults in this adaptive group considered themselves the political leaders for organized social protest in the city at large.

People of Central America, on the other hand, constitute a very small percent of the total Hispano population in Secoya. They may speak the same language as Mexican people and live next door to them but they usually interact very little in social groups.

Reasons for people's ability to participate in the mainstream system may go beyond the number of years that they have spent in the US. That is, although some people in Secoya were recent immigrants from Mexico, they were familiar with the way that the US system operated because they spent many years visiting relatives in Secoya or in other parts of California before they immigrated. Others lived in remote villages and had little if any contact with anyone in the US before immigrating. However, some people lived in the remote villages but had relatives from Secoya, who visited them on the average of once or twice a year over a period of several years. There were also many other families who had never spent any time in the US and only had second-hand knowledge about what to expect as residents in this country. The ability of Mexican immigrants to learn the mainstream culture and to participate confidently in it may have been influenced by how informed they are about the US before immigrating.

Social service and political organizations in Secoya differentiated as to whom they served. One group provided social services primarily to the Central American population while another targeted Mexican groups. A vocal political community group, 'Hispanos Unidos', focused their efforts on issues of the people of Mexican descent (although the name 'Hispanos

Unidos' was selected to attract people from both Mexican and Central American heritage). Their major fundraiser was a 'Cinco De Mayo' fair which raised money for scholarships. Essentially, the groups rarely overlapped in their community social affiliation. They were not hostile by any means, but the division encouraged a tie to one's own cultural group, which promoted cultural maintenance.

Some Hispano youths identified themselves as *Cholos*. The Mexican parents' worst nightmare was that their children would become Cholos. The fear Mexican parents projected about their children becoming Chicano/Hispano became more pronounced at the junior and high school levels, as overt evidence of their group identity intensified. Adults often viewed young Hispanos as antisocial elements in the community. The more traditional Mexicans perceived Cholos as rebellious and defiant while counselors who worked with them in the community center described them as teenagers who encountered racial and language conflicts in the schools. As a result, the young people search for a way to identify themselves that is different from both the Anglo mainstream society and traditional family beliefs. Hispano youths, however, recognized their dilemma as social conflict when they attend Anglo-dominant schools. Adult Hispano community leaders at the Secoya Community Center assist Hispano youths in organizing social projects. Young Hispanos found it necessary to form alliances to provide the identity base they seek wanted for themselves.

However, the youths' parents, who also considered themselves to be Hispanos, viewed their children's actions as deviant from the traditional ways. If children faced problems in school because of their dress and their peer-group behavior, parents found it increasingly difficult to contend with their children's changing dynamics in the family. Systematic assistance to families on how to deal with their children's academic and social problems was mostly absent.

The label Mexican American identified people who may not be as politically active as other long-tenured people of Mexican heritage. Families of Mexican heritage who had lived in the United States for many generations identified with Hispanos as noted above but chose to label themselves as Mexican

American. Subtle yet notable differences exist in some contexts. While children of recent Mexican arrivals tended to be primarily Spanish proficient, children of Mexican American parents tend to be more English proficient, and on occasion proficient in both languages if they have participated in an exceptional bilingual program. This language distinction created an ethnic boundary at times, since many immigrant families disliked the idea of their children associating with Mexican Americans who had 'lost' their language and culture. Because language is an important source of cultural identity, it is used for the purpose of understanding the dynamics of ethnicity within Secoya.

Mexican Americans consider themselves well adapted socially and economically to the demands of the mainstream society. In turn, they viewed immigrant Mexicans as a lower class of workers. The economic distinctions were apparent in dress, home, employment, and language. Mexican Americans were apt to be property owners and more financially able to dress according to middle class fashion's dictates. Mexican Americans born in this country prided themselves on having learned the English language and customs sufficiently well to work in what they consider 'professional' jobs. Many had moved from blue-collar jobs to pink- or white-collar positions.

The majority of the Mexican sector in Secoya immigrated from Aguililla, Michoacan or other smaller towns in that vicinity, such as Apatzingan. Families from Michoacan have continued to arrive in a steady flow of immigration for the past thirty years and have become the largest groups in Secoya. Some immigrated as undocumented workers and found employment in restaurants, nearby industry, and domestic work in order to earn enough money to establish legal residency. Once immigrants become permanent residents, they consider themselves Mexican Americans and made a strong effort to learn English and to enlist in job-training classes to learn a trade. Other immigrants from Central American countries including El Salvador and Nicaragua co-existed with Mexican immigrants in Secoya. Job skills of the Central American immigrants were assessed by some community job placement officers as more developed than those of Mexican immigrants who generally lived in remote rural areas in Mexico. The job market, however, constrained even the skilled workers to low-paying temporary positions.

In addition to preserving the language bond, Mexican parents wanted their children to maintain cultural practices which ensure cohesion within the entire Spanish-speaking community. Some traditional religious holidays are observed by the Sacred Heart Church which was almost adjacent to Gardner School. The Spanish-speaking community in Secoya generally celebrated such religious days as *El Día de la Virgen de Guadalupe*, and All Saints' Day (November 1). Baptisms, weddings, *quinceneras* (a social debut/religious celebration for 15-year-old girls) and first communions remained popular celebrations for many Mexican Americans in varying degrees depending on their financial situations. On January 6th (*El Día de los Reyes Magos*) some Mexican children still placed their shoes outside their windows in hopes that *los reyes magos*, (the 'Three Kings') would fill them with gifts. Parents tried to fulfill their children's wishes even if it meant placing only a few pieces of candy in their shoes. Some traditions were discontinued as Mexican American families in Secoya replaced them with other celebrations: Halloween instead of *Dia de los Muertos* and giving gifts at Christmas along with their peers rather than waiting for the Reyes Magos. Discontinuing traditional practices also occurred when it became inconvenient. For example, couples married in traditional Catholic ceremonies use special cushions to kneel on during the church ceremony. If local stores do not carry these items or if they could not find someone to make them, the couples are forced to change tradition, eliminating that feature of the ceremony.

The language boundary between Spanish-speaking and non-Spanish-speaking Mexican Americans was blurred in the case of Mexican American parents who expect their children to learn English and maintain Spanish. Children of Mexican immigrant families were strongly encouraged to maintain Spanish for the purpose of family cohesion, even after they learned English. This caused some immigrant families to advocate bilingual-bicultural education programs. Although the more recent Mexican immigrants spoke more proficient Spanish than Mexican American children who were several generations removed from Mexico, both groups of the community desired to have their children retain Spanish as demonstrated by its use at home.

A bilingual-bicultural education program existed at Gardner and Oakgrove Elementary Schools, providing instruction in English and Spanish for the limited English proficient students. The program at one point had been centralized and coordinated by an administrator in the central office; however, since the California bilingual law ceased to be enforced when it expired, the schools in the Secoya School District were left to their own devices to provide bilingual instruction to Spanish-speaking students. There are State Department requirements which the school districts should implement in providing primary language instruction to the school districts. Largely, however, the local school district governing body was entrusted with decisions concerning the education of limited-English-speakers. For example, Oakgrove school, with a high number of Spanish-speaking students, began a successful whole language program to help Spanish-speaking students learn to read in Spanish and English. Although three children in this study attended Oakgrove school, they were not involved in that program since the program was not operative during the span of this project. Gardner and Neil schools, however, had not been involved in any major experimentation with new programs at the time we collected data. However, Contreras and Delgado–Contreras (in press) provided important insights into the ways that Mexican American families in Gardner school participated in their children's schooling. While many Mexican American families are not highly visible in traditional school activities such as the Parent/Teacher Association (PTA), they held strong values for their children to achieve. Within the limitations of their material resources, they gave their children a desk or place to study, and most importantly, they provide guidance and verbal moral support to encourage them to learn.

How people live in their community, how they define themselves ethnically, how they respond to sociopolitical pressures from mainstream groups in the community all contribute to the organization of family. To the extent that parents attempt to maintain their values and language while learning new skills and taking advantage of available resources to obtain better employment, children develop a world view of their community, the services and opportunities available, and the 'know how' to acquire them. The specifics are observable through direct interaction among family members in their households and the way in which those beliefs, values and skills are reflected by children in their interactions with peers.

Studying the Sociocultural Context of Learning

The family's sociocultural practices in the home and community influence the children's performance in the classroom. The research focuses on eleven families and four major issues related to the children in these families: 1) the patterns of children's behavior in specific social contexts, 2) the socialization processes in home and classroom tasks and play events, 3) the sociocultural changes of language and interaction practices between the three settings and, 4) the cultural accommodation and effective classroom instruction necessary to enhance learning for Spanish-speaking children.

As we observed how children received and participated in the culture at home and at school, we noted the manner in which children modeled and recreated the rules transmitted by adults. Culture is a dynamic process. Children are not merely passive recipients, they learn the rules and change them. In addition, culture changes constantly through contact with other cultures and through changes in the structural forces of the society. For example, a variety of factors affect family structure. Women have not always had an active role in the work force. Economic demands on the family have forced both men and women to work outside the home, thus changing family relations (Wald, Evans, Smrekar, and Ventresca, 1989). Increasing numbers of single parent households also reflect some of the major cultural changes which affect kinship relations and roles. Another major determinant in shaping family networks is the adult role in the work force (Segura, 1989). Groups that occupy the lowest strata in the work force usually have less access to opportunities that are readily available to those in higher paying positions, such as travel and contact with politically influential people. Experiences differ, and cultural norms in the home often reflect limited socioeconomic opportunities in the macro society.

The social context of interactions was examined in various settings to construct the sociocultural, linguistic and cognitive patterns of learning. Events were organized into respective settings and comparisons drawn among them. Sociocultural patterns of interactions were identified and described within the organizing patterns. We can then understand the cultural rules of the three domains, the family, the play arena and the classroom, and determine potential educational implications at the lesson level of the instructional program.

This research was an extension of a smaller study on issues of continuity and discontinuity conducted with four families (Delgado-Gaitan, 1983). At least one parent of the eleven families selected to participate in this study attended an adult night English as a Second Language class. All but one of the households were two-parent families. The fourteen children in the eleven families selected for the study played together because they knew each other from school or religious instruction in the local church. The play cohorts made it possible to study interaction in and out of school. The children were all enrolled in one of the three elementary schools: Gardner, Oakgrove or Neil. Children interactions in the bilingual primary grades (first through third grades) and a non-bilingual fourth grade were observed in these three elementary schools. An early elementary grade perspective was intentional so as to ascertain the developmental aspects of children's activities during a period when language and literacy are particularly critical in the formal setting.

Observations of home, play and classroom activities required a systematic yet flexible routine. Although children followed a similar routine in their play and home activities sometimes it was necessary to spend long periods of time with them in settings outside of the classroom to capture the spontaneous nature of their activities. Classroom lessons were more predictable because formal education settings tend to operate according to a predesigned curriculum. Each classroom, home and play activity appeared to have a sequential framework which

Table 2.1   Profile of children and families

Child's name	Grade level	Reading level[2]	Children per family	Parents' years of schooling[3]	
				Mother	Father
Marina Martinez	4	3	6	4	6
Raul Martinez[1]	2	1	6	4	6
Mona Martinez[1]	2	K	6	4	6
Marcos Solis[1]	4	3	4	6	0
Sonia Solis[1]	2	3	4	6	0
Rosa Segura	3	3	2	2	9
Mario Reyes	3	1	3	4	4
Saul Cortez	3	4	3	6	6
Alicia Alva	3	4	2	9	6
Adriana Baca	2	1	2	3	–
Jesus Gomez	1	1	2	6	6
Maria Ramirez	2	1	4	4	6
Ramona Mesa	3	4	2	6	6
Tomas Soto	2	3	3	5	4

Notes: 1   The Martinez and the Solis are siblings.
2   Reading levels were based on teachers' evaluations.
3   Parents' education took place in Mexico.

included a beginning, an event and a closure. We also conducted interviews with adults in the home and school settings. Observations and interviews were audio recorded and transcribed. Data were collected over a three-year period. In the analysis, we examined the sociocultural nature of the activities in which children interacted according to the personnel involved, the roles and status of the participants and the goals of those engaged in the process.

For the researchers, initial contact in the target community was critical, since it established the quality and mood of the working relationship between the researchers and the participants. By observing the community we were able to ascertain the daily life of the people, the businesses in the community, the public language of the people, the community social services and the leaders, and the schools, thus understanding the interactions of families in the larger community setting.

The demographic data were verified by interviews with community people who provided a historical perspective of people of Mexican heritage residing in Secoya. They were invaluable sources in helping to formulate a cultural history of

Secoya from the arrival of the first immigrants from Michoacan through their varied adaptation to mainstream culture.

The research approach in this study made personal contact with community members essential. In planning for the research, we included developing a trusting relationship with the children and their families not only because ethnography mandates it but also because of the fear for children's welfare in this day and age. This established the quality and mood of the working relationship between the researcher and the participants.

The first contacts in the community were with older members of the community who had a historical perspective of the immigration of Mexicans into Secoya. Informants who had lived in Secoya for over twenty years were interviewed.

Only one class in Neil school was not a bilingual classroom. The schools were selected because the children in the study attended there. The teachers were contacted and assured that the study was not an evaluation of their teaching but would focus on the way in which children interacted with their peers and with the teacher.

The cases presented in this study are by no means representative of all Mexican American students in the state of California or other states across the US nor is it the intent of ethnography to generalize, although children and families share certain characteristics within and across communities. Understanding the processing of change is only possible through face-to-face interaction over an extended period of time. The study is a close-up of children's learning processes in and out of school, driven by the need to understand how Mexican American children in a particular community learn to belong in their culture and change within it as they accommodated to a new culture. The study of Mexican American children's learning activities has significance for many other children with comparable backgrounds under similar conditions. Statistics demonstrating just how much schools have failed Mexican-American students underlie the urgent call for research to help us understand the interplay of cognitive processes and cultural activity. Activities in the community, e.g. grocery shopping, reveal a set of complex computational strategies; organizing players in a game sheds light on children's leadership ability. Children may perform successfully in extracurricular activities but may find school-like tasks difficult which, in fact, are not harder. Cultural change from home to school for Mexican American children depends largely on the corresponding activities which produce changes in their immediate environment. That is, change at a level of culture or of group values which does not produce corresponding changes in activity is not likely to change patterns of thought in children. It therefore becomes important to examine children's activities in different settings to understand how they are organized to determine how activities in the classroom can be shaped to maximize learning.

Chapter 3

Socialization in the Home

The socialization process in the home involves the transmission of values imbedded in the social context from the parents to the children (Kohn, 1983). Household chores provide one aspect of the complex process through which children interact with parents and siblings. Observing the children as they do their household chores enabled us to understand how children act in the family and how they helped to organize and support their household. Language and sociocultural norms that governed family interaction in the home became evident when children engaged in activities around the home. Although parents and children share an intimate relationship in the privacy of their home, parents spend much of their time away from home if they are employed or have responsibilities like running and dealing with other institutions in the community. Parents expected their children to contribute to the operation of the household since the adults' work hours were long, making it difficult to maintain a clean house and watch over the younger children. In most families, children were familiar with routine chores from the time they were able to understand directions.

Family Life and Household Rules

Among the families in this study, household chores were assigned to children according to their age. Children younger than 6 or 7 were expected to keep the house clean by picking up papers when directed by their elders. They also put away or got items requested by parents. By 6 or 7 years of age, children were expected to undertake more responsibility in the home, including dish-washing, sweeping, emptying the garbage, taking care of younger siblings, running errands to the store, and other outdoor chores.

In most cases, the parents stated that their children helped at home and obeyed those norms made explicit to them. Although each family set their own rules for the household, some common rules existed across families: children had to get permission from parents to leave the home, children had to obey adults' commands, and children were expected to get along without fighting.

To ensure safety, parents insisted that children request permission before going to friends' homes. Consequences for disobeying this rule varied from reminding children of the rule to spanking them when they returned home. The Martinez family was less rigid about this rule since both parents worked from 5 a.m. to 6 p.m. Their children had a great deal of freedom but were expected to be home when parents returned from work. In the other families that participated in this study one parent was usually home, making it easier to enforce the home rules.

Parents required children to obey adult instructions in all cases. Children's appropriate behavior was rewarded and infractions were punished. Being obedient meant not talking back to adults. One parent expressed his view as follows: 'Yo quiero que mi hijo sea bien educado — que no sea grosero.' (I want my child to be well educated — not to be rude.) 'Ser bien educado' had many connotations, but fundamentally it implied being respectful toward others, especially elders. Part of the obedience and respect rule was demonstrated through still another explicit rule: no fighting. Parents insisted that they wanted their children to get along. 'Que no peleen,' (that they don't fight), reflected the parents' expectations about the way that children should behave with each other. In practice, children were not usually physically aggressive with each other, but they were quick to assert their rights verbally, even including verbal dueling. On some occasions fierce looks and facial gestures accompanied the verbal challenges. We observed the 'No pelear,' (don't fight) rule being taxed. On the other hand, children did not resort to physical aggression, so they did not interpret it as fighting. They were merely 'disgustados,' (upset). Thus, they did not violate the house rules.

Family Setting

Three of the families in this study had immigrated from Mexico City and Tijuana and El Salvador. The others immigrated to the United States from Michoacan. Apatzingan and Aguililla were the more common cities of origin in Michoacan. In some cases, although Apatzingan and Aguililla were the nearest cities to the ranches where the families lived, the ranches were a long distance from the cities. Most families immigrated prior to 1975.

Education for all but two of the parents ended long before they completed elementary school in Mexico. Two of the parents, Mr. Segura and Mrs. Alva, had completed the equivalent of high school in Mexico. English language-speaking skills were limited for most parents in the study. Mr. Alva spoke more English than the other adults; he attributed this accomplishment to having studied it in night school for seven years, since he arrived in the United States. He spoke only Spanish at home. Parents found that they did not need much English in the jobs they secured but they did need it to advance to other positions. For example, they could work in the assembly line without skills in English because people in supervisory capacity were usually bilingual, but in order to obtain supervisory positions, English was required. Mr. Alva had learned the reality of the language issue relative to positions. He was determined to become a supervisor in the gardening position he held. He was willing to make the additional sacrifice to attend night school to learn English. His wife had encouraged him because she knew the importance of furthering his education since she had completed high school in Mexico. English, for her, however, was more difficult than for him, so they decided that the whole family should support him to pursue learning English. Almost all the parents had attended night school to learn English but they had not been systematic in their effort. For about one year, seven of these families attended classes offered in Gardner school for parents to achieve literacy in Spanish and English as a Second Language while learning how to help their children to do their homework. Some parents were more sytematic about learning English than others but generally they felt that they had to make some effort to continue learning the language in order to help their children even if they could not advance in their employment.

All of the families had resided in Secoya for over five years and the target children in the study began kindergarten in Gardner school. The families lived near each other. The Reyes, Segura and Solis families lived in one apartment complex, the Baca, Soto, Mesa, and Cortez families lived in small single houses on the same street as the apartment complex. The Martinez and Gomez families lived in a different fourplex apartment house. The Alva and the Ramirez families lived on different streets within two blocks of the others. Some families shared their small houses with family members who had immigrated from Mexico but who could not yet afford a separate house. Temporary jobs and other financial constraints also forced families into sharing a house.

The larger houses had a bit of a yard where children could play, but when there was no play yard, children used the carport or driveway to gather. If the houses had sufficiently large back yards, families kept rabbits and chickens. The chickens provided fresh eggs for the family and the rabbits were raised to become meals for special occasions.

The apartment fourplex consisted of three single-bedroom apartments on the second level over the carports and one was on the lower level. A small patch of grass surrounded a single tree next to the driveway. An electronic plant and a tool and die garage were located in the residential area along with small marketplaces and specialty boutiques nearby.

Places of employment were at the dry flower company where flower arrangements were made and at a restaurant food supplier that made and packaged food for restaurants. In addition, parents had to work on Saturdays as gardeners or in other small free lance jobs. Parents, when possible, alternated work shifts and shared childcare.

Table 3.1. *Parents, age, years in the US, occupation, literacy and language proficiency*

Family name	Age		English oral language proficiency[1]		Reading proficiency by grade level equivalent[2]				Spanish writing skills by grade level		English writing skills by grade level		Years in US as residents		Occupation	
					Spanish		English									
	Mother	Father	Mother	Father	Mother	Father	Mother	Father	Mother	Father	Mother	Father	Mother	Father	Mother	Father
Martinez	36	40	1	3	3	6	1	2	2	5	1	2	8	10	Electronic manufacture worker	Electronic manufacture worker
Solis	30	32	3	2	4	1	2	0	4	0	1	1	8	8	Miscellaneous. Part-time	Electronic manufacture worker. Gardener
Segura	25	28	2	4	4	12	3	7	4	12	3	6	7	7	Electronic manufacture worker	Electronic manufacture worker
Reyes	27	28	2	3	6	8	1	4	5	7	1	2	5	8	Miscellaneous. Part-time	Mechanic. Musician (weekends)
Cortez	43	45	1	3	1	7	5	8	1	6	0	3	7	7	Domestic worker	Carpenter
Alva	28	35	3	5	12	12	3	8	12	12	4	7	10	10	Receptionist	Gardener
Baca	28	—	4	—	6	—	3	—	5	—	3	—	10	—	Domestic worker	—
Gomez	35	40	3	2	4	3	2	5	3	3	2	1	5	5	Electronic manufacture worker	Tool & die machinist
Ramirez	33	38	3	4	4	6	2	5	5	5	2	5	6	13	Cobbler shoe repair	Cobbler shoe repair
Mesa	27	35	2	4	5	6	6	2	5	5	1	3	7	7	Electronic manufacture worker	Electronic manufacture worker
Soto	38	40	4	3	6	4	6	4	6	4	5	1	12	12	Waitress	Cook

Notes: 1 English oral proficiency was assessed by the IDEA–kit levels 1–8 in listening, word, sentence, fluency with 1 being least proficient and 8 most proficient.
2 Levels resulted from TESL and Spanish tests given adult education classes. Other information was obtained through ethnographic interviews.

Another place of employment was a toy company, where adults assembled toy parts in the production line. They earned a little more than minimum wage per hour. Some adults had seniority in the company, which made their employment some-what more secure than others who had only temporary status. However, seniority in the company made little difference if their company moved the business to a different location as had happened to some families.

When one of the companies moved thirty miles away from Secoya, the transfer created a great deal of inconvenience for entire families. Some of the families did not have a car, so they depended on car pool rides or took the bus to work. The work day was extended by at least three hours if the parents had to take the bus; they did not return home until after 6:00 p.m. Transportation problems meant that the children had to assume more responsibility for themselves around the house, from get-ting themselves to school to preparing their own meals and cleaning house. Long work hours also occurred when parents had to work more than one job as a financial necessity.

Parental absence made it easier for the children to sleep in and ignore their school obligations. School absences were fre-quent for a couple of the children, in particular Raul and Adriana who chose to stay home and play rather than attend school. Teachers had a difficult time reaching parents who worked late hours to report about the absences and the fact that the children were behind in their work. Parents, on the other hand, assumed that all was well because they complied with what they perceived as their parental responsibility to provide their children with moral support to stay in school. Thus, they did not contact the school unless the school personnel contacted them.

Long work days also made it difficult for parents to go to the laundromat as often as necessary and children sometimes missed school if they did not have clean clothes available. Although small items of clothing were washed in the bathtub, it was insufficient for the family needs. Families who had the support of relatives who lived-in managed to deal a bit better with the care of the family and the household.

These families represented a cohort who had immigrated

and was attempting to adjust in a fast-paced society. Although they faced employment constraints as a result of their limited educational and job skills, they pursued positions that would benefit their families. The sacrifices to learn a new language in a new country were made because they believed that their children could have better education and economic opportunities in the United States than in Mexico.

Cultural changes were the most difficult for parents to contend with. They felt that it was more difficult to raise children in the United States because the language and customs were different from those in Mexico. While they appreciated the fact that in Secoya many of the businesses and services were bilingual, their children were learning a language they did not know and they observed them becoming more rebellious and disrespectful than they had expected. Mr. Ramirez's fear, for example, was that their children would become involved with drugs.

> Yo quiero que Jesús estudie para que tenga un empleo mejor que el mío. Yo temo que con las escuela tan libres como son, que mi hijo va a comenzar a tomar drogas y eso sería muy triste. Nosotros le hablamos y tratamos de convencerlo que es por su bien que siga estudiando y que se cuide de amistades malas.

> (I want to see Jesus study so that he can have a better job than I have. But, I fear that with the schools as liberal as they are now, that my son will begin to take drugs and that would be very sad. We talk to him and try to convince him that it is for his own good that he continue studying and to stay away from bad friends.)

School was important to these families so that their children could take advantage of employment opportunities in the future.

Family Life and Children's Daily Routine

Parents established codes of behavior to manage their family during their absence. For the most part, they emphasized orderliness of the home and compatibility with family members. The girls seemed to assume much of the responsibility around the house particularly in indoor household tasks. Boys were relegated more responsibility when they were the oldest in the family. Both boys and girls were expected to be more self-sufficient during the parents' long work day.

Men considered the women primarily responsible for managing the home. Although the three room apartment was not large, women found that cleaning up after the children was constant work. Children reluctantly accepted many of the tasks assigned by the parents. Usually the oldest children were assigned most of the tasks around the house.

According to Mr. Soto, teaching correct values to the children was the most important function of the family. At the beginning of the study the Soto children, Tomás and Manuela, experienced slightly different expectations in their home as compared to those of children in the other three families. The most that was expected of Tomás and Manuela was that they not mess up the house, or as said by Tomás, 'No debemos de hacer travesuras' (We are not to be mischievous). Mr. and Mrs. Soto felt that 8–year–old Tomás should help out but that his primary concern should be his homework and attending school.

Generally, on weekdays, the day began at about 6:00 a.m. in these households. Parents awakened to feed the youngest in the family. By the time children got to be 7 or 8 years old, they were expected to feed themselves before going to school. Children woke up about 7:00 a.m., dressed, washed, and went into the kitchen and often helped with younger children.

For example, when the Solis' left for work, Marcos assumed responsibility and poured Sonia and himself a glass of milk, then sat two bowls and a box of cereal on the table. If parents worked alternate shifts, one parent slept in and the other left for work. The parent that arrived home from the graveyard shift took responsibility for the breakfast while the other slept or got up and cared for the baby in those households where there was a young child. In some families, children were responsible for sweeping, washing dishes, and making beds. These tasks often had to be done before the children left for school.

At 8:00 a.m. children usually began walking to school.

They picked up friends along the way if they lived on the same street. Many children from other apartments on the same block walked to school at the same time. When siblings went into school at the same time, they walked to school together. On occasion, the boy siblings rode their bikes to school and the girls walked. Gardner School was only about one and one-half blocks from their neighborhood. The children walked half a block down, turned right on the next street and after one short block they entered the school playground.

Siblings did not always walk home together, even though they got out of school at the same time. Marcos, for example, never stopped off anywhere, while Sonia sometimes stopped at her friend's apartment, even though both were expected to go straight home. When they arrived home, Mr. Solis was in the house with baby Sabrina. Whether Marcos and Sonia stayed inside depended on the weather. A popular afternoon activity was watching 'Batman' on television. The boys sometimes went to other boys' houses to watch television. If some mothers were home in the afternoon they had primary rights to the television. When Mrs. Solis was home, for example, she watched her soap opera in Spanish as she crocheted dresses for her baby. Sonia either stayed with her mother and Sabrina or visited Rosa next door.

Children varied their after-school activities. Sometimes they stayed in the house, theirs or a friend's, and watched television together. Like the Solis', the three Martinez children did not always walk home together after school. Mona was the most consistent about going straight home. Marina often stopped at her friend's house for an hour before going home, while Raul visited friends who lived two blocks away.

Parents' Economic and Educational Concerns

Parents were quick to point out that a one bedroom apartment or house was less than adequate for a five-member family. Space alone was not the issue; landlords often neglected the tenants' complaints. In one of the homes, part of the front window was broken and a few months passed before the owner replaced it.

A wall and ceiling damaged by running water and a leaky faucet inside the apartment also awaited the owner's attention. The family's inability to purchase furniture was due largely to frequent unemployment.

Financial instability for some of the families usually restricted the family's diet to beans, corn tortillas, and milk. Once a week they had some type of meat. Only two of the families, the Seguras and the Alvas, seemed to be financially capable of a higher standard of living. The Reyes and the Baca families were on the other end of the continuum where they could not afford a telephone, or a birthday cake for the children's birthdays. On his birthday, Mario came home from school and stayed inside the apartment because he did not want to tell any of his friends that his family could not afford to celebrate it.

The reason many parents wanted their children to help around the house was that they expected them to contribute to the routine of the household by performing chores. Parents imposed a code of conduct which reinforced obedience and collaboration. As Mrs. Solis explained: 'Estos niños necesitan aprender a trabajar — si no, salen flojos sinvergüenzas y no consiguen un buen trabajo.' (These children need to know how to work, if not, they will be a lazy good for nothing and they will not get good jobs.)

When children spent time alone after school they kept busy with activities such as watching cartoons, cuddling their dolls on the porch of the apartments or dressing up in heels and grown-up clothes. Mario and Tomás preferred to be alone more than the other children. They spent a great deal of time inside their respective apartments even when the other children were outdoors. Mario often stayed inside to avoid confrontations with children who teased him. He had continuous conflicts with friends because he called the girls offensive names, but at other times they all played together.

From going to the store to just walking to neighbors to smell the roses, children sought companionship of their friends for play. One of their favorite pastimes was storytelling. Vivid imagination was also reflected in their creative drawings.

Some children were expected to help with the childcare after school. The older children usually took the younger siblings along to their play activities. At other times, they played with other children on their street or in the apartment complex. Mariana, Adriana's 4-year-old sister, received a great deal of attention from the children when they got home from school. They cuddled and teased her. She willingly played with all the neighbors too. On occasion, Adriana took Mariana to Mona's house to visit since she lived only one and one-half blocks away. The girls enjoyed playing chase around the house with the younger girl. Neither parents nor children ever mentioned that taking care of the younger siblings was a required task, yet older children were always caring for their younger siblings. Families considered being with one another a natural part of belonging to the family. Children, therefore, did not resent childcare as much as they did other tasks. Often Sonia and Marcos were left alone to care for their younger siblings when their father had gone to work and their mother had not yet arrived.

Most children's activities involved various ages since their younger siblings often joined them in play or household chores. Tomás and Raul sometimes preferred to join their older brothers; they liked to imitate the older high school boys who joined with the Cholo youth group. The boys typically wore khaki pants, Pendleton shirts and head bands. They frequented the community center front area and listened to rap music on large console portable radios. Although Spanish was their dominant language, English rock music and 'oldies' were played by some of the older boys. Occasionally, they spoke English to each other, especially when talking about their friends or music. Tomás and Raul did not dress like the the older boys when they hung out with them, and usually arrived home around four or five o'clock, shortly before their parents arrived home from work.

Disciplinary Practices

Parents had more discipline problems with the older boys and sometimes girls who took up membership in cholo groups. Problems ranged from disrespectful language to ignoring household responsibilities. Parents admitted that they dealt differently with some of their children than with others. Mrs. Cortez, felt that she had to be more strict with her daughter Olga than with her son Saul becaue Olga was stubborn and rebellious. Mrs. Martinez also believed her younger daughter Mona needed more disciplining than her oldest daughter, Marina. She had to order Mona several times to take a bath before she listened while Marina did not need reminding. Mona often tried to negotiate taking her bath on another day.

Children were made aware of their tasks and responsibilities through frequent reminders. Dishwashing received most votes for the least popular chore around the house. Most of the children who had to do dishes emphatically expressed their dislike for it. Occasionally children who did not always have a daily assignment to wash dishes actually volunteered as a way to win their parents' favor.

Parental permission was one family rule that most children did not easily disobey. When children feared that they would not receive permission to visit friends they went anyway. Infraction of the rules usually meant that children were punished by not being allowed to visit their friends. Within the same family one sibling would adhere more to the parents' rules than the others. The child whom the parents held to be most responsible usually followed the parents' dictates whereas the siblings who were considered irresponsible by the parents broke the house rules more often. Some children knew that their parents were displeased and while they resented the criticisms they agreed that they would rather play than do household chores.

The type of household chore assigned to children rested in the enforcement of their respective family responsibilities. A partial reason for the disparity may be that the some families lived in a very confined three-room apartment which did not require much upkeep while other families like the Alvas, Gomez and the Martinez had a two- or three-bedroom house with a yard which required more care.

In the evening when the parents arrived home from work during the weekdays, the children were expected to be home. Following a short rest, women prepared dinner while some fathers spent time with the children in the living room. At least once a week the adults attended church meetings. Several of the families were involved in weekly Bible reading classes at the Sacred Heart Catholic Church which was around the corner from Gardner School. Some read the Bible to the children at home and talked to them about the lessons to be learned. Mrs. Martinez read stories about the life of Jesus. The children were very interested in the stories and often requested her to sit and share them. Parents wanted to inculcate moral values in their children.

Family standards for the children were quite similar. Parents expected children to be obedient, respectful, and helpful around the house. Mr. Reyes, for example, emphatically stated, 'Todos tienen que ser parejos. Que no perjudiquen a nadie. Desear más es una mala costumbre.' (Everybody has to be equal. Not to hurt anyone. It is bad manners to want more.)

The children were quite aware of the consequences of not observing the guidelines: they would not receive spending money and might even get a scolding. Most parents concurred that spanking did not accomplish much, and they sometimes became exasperated when the children did not behave. Parents in three of the households relied largely on their church Bible group to assist them with their discipline problems. Through religion, parents transmitted the value of patience and respect as illustrated in the incident which transformed their oldest son, Ramon, as related by Mrs. Martinez.

Over a period of a year Ramon made a complete turn-around in his attitude about material goods. For a long time, Ramon insisted on owning a large radio console. We sacrificed to give him some money. Ramon even took a part-time job as a mechanic's assistant at Pablo's Car Mechanic on Las Terrazas road. He saved his money for radios which cost over one hundred dollars each. Both were stolen within a week after he bought them. He was quite depressed following each of the incidents. One day he realized that the money he earned should go toward a washer for the family instead of for radios. He felt badly for the sacrifice we made each weekend carrying the wash to the laundromat located a block from

Sacred Heart Church. And I know that his change of heart was due to the Bible readings.

The children's daily routine of housework and play activities varied minimally on weekends. Occasionally, fathers took their children fishing to Half Moon Bay when the weather was warm, sometimes the mothers took them shopping to a major department store which was about two miles away. Most often, however, the children and parents stayed home while men went to their Saturday gardening jobs. On such days, children were forced to stay home unless an uncle or their grandmother came to take them to their house. Financial constraint was the reason parents gave for not taking the children on any outings during the weekends. They compensated the children for any tasks by giving them a quarter for ice cream or buying them cakes which were rationed out for as long as they lasted.

On Saturdays a member of the 'Movimento Familia' from Sacred Heart Catholic Church came to the homes to ask how many would need to be picked up for Mass on Sunday. Sometimes the children went, but most often they declined. If they chose to go to church, it became their primary activity. Children were picked up by the church bus to attend Mass, then stayed for religious instruction to prepare them for first communion or confirmation; they stayed in church at least three hours. Some adults attended Mass at San Miguel Catholic Church on San Jose Street, about one mile from the neighborhood in the opposite direction from Sacred Heart. Certain weekends were reserved for married couples' retreats called *Cursillos*.

The remainder of their Sunday was usually uneventful. They watched television programs on a Spanish-speaking channel, such as *Siempre en Domingo*, a variety program, or played in and around the apartment. Occasionally, the Martinez children went to their aunt's house which was close to the downtown area of the adjacent incorporated city.

Extended family played an crucial role for these families. Grandparents, aunts and uncles helped out in childcare, finances, disciplining of children and other personal family matters. For example, the Seguras shared a close relationship with the grand-mother. Many weekends and weekday evenings were spent at her house. Mrs. Segura, being the oldest daughter, assumed a great deal of responsibility for her 15-year-old sister, Berta, and her brother, also a teenager, which meant that she advised the younger siblings in decisions about school and marriage. Some-times Laura and Rosa played records and danced with her oldest cousin. Other times they played with the neighbors' children. Families who had grandparents in Secoya spent a good part of every weekend with them. The grandparents' house became the central meeting place to share food, talk and insights.

Indoor and Outdoor Chores

Children participated in the general maintenance activities around the house. The indoor tasks, such as washing dishes, sweeping, and cooking, were usually performed by the women and girls, while outdoor chores, such as feeding chickens and cleaning the yard, tended to be taken care of by the male family members. At times there was an overlap of these chores. Marina was home more often that the older brothers, so she was often assigned the tasks of running errands and washing the outside steps. Another reason that much of the responsibility rested on the oldest girl in the family is that her older brother usually did not help with work indoors. He preferred to play his radio in his room. Since he was the ultimate authority in the parents' ab-sence, he got away with doing little work. The fathers usually disciplined the older boys.

Parents trusted that children would request assistance if they did not understand the chore assigned to them. They honored children's requests for clarification during the task. Sometimes when carrying out an activity the parents had to coach the children step by step not because the children request-ed it but because the parents wanted the task done especially well and to ensure the child's safety. On a Saturday afternoon, Mrs. Baca and her daughter illustrated this point: Mrs. Baca requested Adriana to help her warm tortillas for the family's lunch so it would be ready quicker since her younger daughter and mother were coming. Adriana accepted graciously and walked into the kitchen. She began by unwrapping a package of tortillas and placing one at a time on the burner. Her mother glanced over and warned her to be careful with the fire, but Adriana had already found a way to protect herself by using a large spoon to turn the tortilla without burning her fingers. Her mother suggested that she put a small bowl of water next to the burner and dip her fingers in once before turning the tortillas so that her fingers would not burn. Adriana cringed and cried out, '¡Ay me da miedo!' (Oh I'm scared!). She proceeded to dip her finger and turn the tortillas asking her mother, '¿Así, mama?' (Like this, mom?) While stirring the pot of soup, her mother glanced over and nodded affirmatively.

The incentive to get Adriana to help was so that lunch would be ready much faster. But, Adriana also received positive praise from her mother for handling a difficult task like turning the tortillas without burning her fingers. Although Adriana seemed to have her own system, she was willing to try her mother's approach which proved successful.

Childcare in the Family

Much like Adriana's family, in the Martinez family almost everyone was expected to help take care of the youngest children. In the Martinez family, whenever parents were not present, children were always supervised by either Francisco, Mr. Martinez's older brother, or their cousin Rebeca. For example, Mona, aged six, was expected to care for Nidia, who was two, even when the parents were home. The mother gave instructions to take Nidia to the bathroom or to care for her outdoors.

The younger brother sometimes seemed to avoid responsibility around the house by spending a great deal of his time with friends away from home. Mr. and Mrs. Martinez recognized that he did not participate around the house as much as others, and they both agreed that sooner he began helping out more at home, the better. Although the parents saw the disparity between the amount of work performed by the girls and the boys, they believed that girls should remain at home while boys were allowed more freedom to leave the house.

In the Ramirez family, for example, Maria assisted her mother with dressing and feeding her younger sister. The rest of the times she watched television or drew pictures. Her illustrations revealed artistic talent. Maria complained that her sisters tore up all her work and that she did not have much private space. On one occasion she checked out a book from the library and hid it so that her sisters would not tear it up. She hid it so well that she forgot where she had put the book and had pay late fees at the public library.

Mrs. Ramirez complained that Maria did not accept direction from her as willingly as she did from her father. Maria undermined her mother's authority at home when requested to perform a chore. Her mother was forced to nag Maria before she took action. Maria enjoyed going to the store for errands because she was usually compensated with a dime or a quarter for sunflower seeds.

Children, for the most part, believed that they complied with their parents' expectations in terms of household chores. Children were quick to enumerate certain norms of behavior which they were required to follow: 'Que no interrumpamos cuando está hablando una persona grande.' (No interrupting when an adult is talking); 'Que no digamos maldiciones ni nos peleemos.' (No bad words and no fighting); 'Que no nos enojemos cuando los papas no tienen dinero para llevarnos a alguna parte.' (Not to get mad when the parents cannot afford to take us places); 'Que no nos quejemos de lo que tenemos que comer.' (Not to complain about what we have to eat). The girls in the Martinez family easily admitted that Raul was lax about helping them. Parents realized that they were not as strict with him as they should be, but as soon as he was a couple of years older, they would hold him more accountable.

Changes in employment for the parents often meant a reorganization in family responsibilities. A case in point was a new job for Mr. and Mrs. Ramirez at a computer chip assembly plant which meant a turning point for Maria; she had to assume added responsibility for Berta. Because Mr. and Mrs. Ramirez worked opposited shifts on the assembly line, there was a half-hour gap between the time that Mr. Ramirez left for work and Mrs. Ramirez arrived home. During this half-hour, Maria was instructed to stay inside and care for Berta. Because of this, the parents' standard rule was that Maria must come home without delay. However, when Mr. Ramirez left for work, Maria usually called Alicia Maria or Marina to babysit with her. On one occasion, Maria had been left alone with Berta when their father went to work. Their mother was not scheduled to arrive for another hour. Maria's only assignment was to take care of her little sister until their mother arrived; she was instructed not to allow anyone in the house. Marina, Mona and Sonia knocked on the door and asked Maria to go out to play. Maria opened the door and informed them that she and her sister had to stay in the apartment until their mother came home. Marina tried to convince her to play with them outside under the carport and said they would all help Maria to care for Berta. Maria declined because she feared that their mother would get mad at her if she found them outside. Marina was persistent and proposed to Maria that she let them in and they could help her to care for Berta and meanwhile they could play.

Maria opened the door and let the three girls in the apartment. Marina, Maria and Sonia sat in the living room and turned on the stereo to listen to Maria's father's records. During this time, the two youngest girls went into Berta and Maria's room and began to jump on the bed and hit each other with pillows. Mona fell off the bed and began to cry which brought the three other girls running into the bedroom. Maria screamed at the girls, '¿Qué están haciendo aqui? Mira cómo tienen la cama. Se va a enojar mamá.' (What are you doing in here? Look at what you've done to the bed. Mom is going to get mad.) Sonia quickly assured Maria that they would help her to fix the bed. All of the girls pitched in and they straightened up the bed and Maria told Berta and Mona to go into the living room. All of the girls went into the living room to watch television. However, Maria, uncomfortable with having all of the girls there, asked them to leave because she did not want her mother to find them all inside the house and revoke her trust. The girls left and Maria and her little sister stayed inside the house and waited for their mother.

Maria claimed that she was learning to take care of the house and that her father had specific rules for what he expected. Mr. Ramirez added, 'Quiero que aprendan a obedecer — si obedecen, les compro todo lo que querian, pero si no me obedecen, entonces ya saben que les pego y no les compro lo que quieren.' (I want them to learn to obey — if they obey I'll buy them whatever they want. But if they don't obey, I'll spank them and won't buy them what they want).

Maria's sense of friendship and companionship prompted her to invite her friends in. However, her sense of responsibility for her childcare assignment made her take action to escort her friends out when the situation got out of control. She wanted to please her mother and to gain her confidence but if her mother found her and Berta outside, Maria feared that she would not trust Maria. Marina and Sonia joined Maria in her caretaking responsibilities. The three girls of different ages combined their efforts to assist Maria in her childcare task but Maria knew that she had to assume leadership in order to maintain her parents' acceptance.

Maria accepted her responsibility seriously and was strict with her sister Berta and expected her to sit still while she cared for her. Maria preferred Berta to observe but not to participate in her activities. Maria clearly understood the consequences for failing to perform her tasks. Her father spanked her if she stepped outside the apartment before her mother arrived.

Collective behavior between children appeared on many different levels and in varying degrees depending on the context. The models children had for collectivity were sometimes explicit when the parents verbally encouraged children to work together; other behaviors were modeled by the parents in the process of conducting their daily tasks.

On a Saturday morning in the Reyes household, Mario's mother insisted that he help her by taking care of his youngest sister and stop watching television. The baby was watching television with him in the living room. She needed her diaper changed and to be given a milk bottle. Mario did not want to get up in the middle of his cartoon and his mother was forced to yell at him from the kitchen with a threat that if he did not help out while she was cleaning the kitchen, she would cancel his television privileges for the rest of the day. He immediately got up from the couch, and picked up his sister and took her into the bedroom to change her diaper. His reluctance to change his sister's diaper represents a common response to an adult command to help out with household chores. Seldom did children defy their parents, but on occasion, they stretched out the task as long as they could without causing the parents to be overtly provoked. This was one case where the parents' patience was tested profoundly.

After changing her diaper, Mario left his sister in the bedroom and came out to the living room to watch television again. The baby's crying which brought his mother out of the kitchen. She confronted Mario with a predictable question, '¿Por qué me haces que te siga diciendo que me ayudes con la niña?' (Why do you make me tell you over and over to help me with the baby?) Then she reminded him again that the baby needed a milk bottle. He begrudgingly got up from the couch and fixed the baby a bottle and took it to her in the bedroom.

Although Mario completed the task, Mario manipulated the situation to gain as much control as he could. The mother, however, held to her power to request assistance around the house from Mario. Parental control and authority was evident in the interaction between Mario and his mother, but children's ability to obstruct and not acquiesce to authority also became apparent. That is, children may respect authority but they also challenge it.

Literacy in the Home

Families used and worked with written text in the home beyond the academic type materials which children's brought from school. While reading itself occupies relatively little of the adults' time on a regular basis, adults, regardless of their reading level, read materials in Spanish and some in English (Delgado-Gaitan, 1987). Letters from family members in Mexico and school bulletins (some in Spanish, others in English) were the most commonly read texts in the home. Fewer households read texts for functional or leisure purposes like instruction manuals, or cooking recipies, newspapers, magazines, story books, and Bibles. In the households where text was not used to conduct daily chores, adults reported that they could get whatever information might be provided by those literacy forms through visual media or by asking someone they knew. That is, if women got a cloth dye for a dress, they were more likely to get a friend to show them how to do the job, rather than read the directions even if they had some literacy skills in English.

Recreational reading for adults was minimal in most households. Where leisure reading was more frequent, they read *fotonovelas* (small romance novels) in Spanish. Mr. Alva, Alicia's father, enjoyed reading history books in English when he had the opportunity to read, but he admitted that his time was limited. However, he liked to read in English as much as possible and he appointed himself as the parent in charge of helping the children to do their homework. Parents liked to read storybooks to their children, although it was infrequent in most families. If children did not bring school texts home, sometimes they bought small storybooks or checked them out from the community library.

Some parents had learned how to read to their children in a night literacy project at Gardner School. In that project, adults were taught to read in Spanish and English using children's materials as well as adult literacy curriculum. Reading to children in the home was stressed. Other parents learned how to read to their children through their volunteer work in the preschool. For example, Mrs. Reyes, when she was not working, took Andrea, her 3-year-old daughter, to Gardner preschool daily. She assisted every Monday at the preschool where her daughter attended when she was not working day shifts. She walked with Mario to school and assisted the preschool teacher for three hours. She claimed that the experience was good for her because it gave her ideas about ways to help her children at home. She tried to implement some of the reading activities with her children. Mario, in particular, really enjoyed his mother reading to them.

On one occasion, while Mario and his younger sister, Andrea sat in the living room couch, Mrs. Reyes picked up the book, *Caperucita Roja* (*Little Red Riding Hood*) and told the children that she would read the book but they had to listen. Mario told her to start reading. She read the story from beginning to end in Spanish. Although she did not ask the children any questions while she read the story, following the story, Mario offered a comment, 'A mí me gusta cuando el lobo trata de engañar a caperucita y ella no lo deja comerse la comida de su abuelita.' (I liked that part where the wolf tries to deceive little Red Riding Hood and doesn't let him eat her grandmother's food). Andrea added to Mario's comment by stating that the wolf did not eat the grandmother. To which Mario responded, 'No, porque un lobo no puede comerse a una persona grande.' (No cause a wolf can't eat a big person).

Using a favorite story in this household, Mrs. Solis provided her children a context in which they could talk about it. Although she did not guide the discussion about the book with specific questions, the children seized the opportunity to comment on their favorite parts. Reading to her children was a way that Mrs. Reyes brought her training from the preschool home.

Children sometimes checked out books in the bilingual library at the community center and read them to each other. As did many of the children, Alicia and her younger brother enjoyed reading books they brought home from the library. She was in the third grade and he in the first grade. Jose occasionally requested that Alicia read to him because he did not yet read fluently. Alicia helped her younger brother read a book.

Both children sat on the floor and Alicia held the book in Spanish entitled, *Jorge El Curioso* (Curious George). Alicia held the book and called Jose's attention to the beginning of the story. He said that he already knew how the story began because he had seen the book in school. Jose looked at Alicia and waited for her to read. She began reading it aloud: 'George lived in the jungle. He liked to watch the people from the trees. He was very curious.' Jose interrupted, to tell her that he knew how curious George was and that he could read the next line read. He pointed at the line and read, 'George saw a big yellow thing and he was curious. . . .' Yes, she acknowledged and then finished the sentence, for him. '. . . The yellow thing was a hat. A man was under the hat.' Alicia continued reading, 'George wanted to wear the hat. The man put George in a sack.' Jose commented that he did not like the way that the man put George in the bag because he probably could not breathe. Then she continued reading the story. 'The man brought George to a new home in a zoo.' At that point, Jose began reading along with Alicia as she read the story to him. He overlapped her reading somewhat by re-stating what she read aloud. She did not appear at all affected by Jose's reading aloud with her and she continued, 'George looked around and he was curious.' Jose smiled at Alicia and commented on what a funny character George was. Alicia read another two pages and before completing the story, she laid the book down on the floor and announced that she was going outside to play. Jose remained sitting on the floor and leafed through the book.

Alicia and Jose shared an activity in which they both played roles according to their level of development. Alicia read and Jose listened. But the children were not just representing their respective levels of reading ability, as was apparent when Jose began reading aloud with Alicia. Given this opportunity to have Alicia read to him, he extended his own ability. Alicia, as the more knowledgeable reader, encouraged his efforts when she acknowledged the sentences he read and then added to Jose's comments about his experience with doctor visits.

This reading activity was characteristic of others observed in the household in that they were not part of the school's homework assignments. As part of the teachers' policy, homework assignments were seldom sent home with the children before they reached the third grade except under unusual circumstances when children had been absent for several days. Thus children and their parents were left to their own devices to organize academic activities.

Children reading a book together was one way that children demonstrated their interest in school-like activities. Families expressed their concern for school in a variety of other ways. Interactions between children and parents about missing school are an example. Teachers attributed some of the children's academic problems to children's absences due to family matters. Some parents kept their children out of school to care for younger siblings for two or three hours at a time when they were unable to find a sitter and the parents had doctor's appointments. Sometimes they took the children with them to doctors' appointments to help translate.

Running Errands

Part of helping with the household responsibilities meant that children had to perform errands for the parents. Children's chores outdoors and away from the house meant even more independence because parents were not available to instruct them during the process.

When Jesus arrived from school, he was sometimes expected to run errands for groceries. Jesus came into the apartment after school and played with Sabrina in the living room. His mother, who was starting dinner in the kitchen, called out to him to stop playing and run to the store for her. She instructed him to go to the store to buy a small bunch of *cilantro* (Chinese parsley). Jesus asked for the money and for directions to find the Chinese parsley in the store. His mother instructed him to look in the section where the lettuce and other vegetables are found. Jesus asked his mother if he could keep the change and his mother agreed to just one quarter and rushed him out the door because she wanted to finish dinner. Before running off to the store, he went next door to his friend's house to invite Tomás to accompany him to the store. Tomás opened the door and called to his mother in the house that he was running to the store with Jesus.

The boys walked through their usual path to the store and stopped to pick up empty pop bottles to sell at the store for a few pennies. After buying the Chinese parsley, the boys returned home, walking much faster. Jesus delivered the parsley to his mother and kept the change.

Although Jesus did not know where to locate the Chinese parsley, his mother's instructions were sufficient for him to complete the task. Companionship was a characteristic feature of children's household tasks even if in many cases there was no direct assistance as was the case of Jesus and Tomás.

Jesus asked for a quarter but actually he kept all the change from the transaction. Jesus and his mother used Spanish throughout the interaction. Jesus exemplified how companionship was sought out when executing a task when he asked Tomás to go with him to the store, and Sonia also offered her companionship. Getting assistance or companionship in performing a task often depended on the availability of friends or siblings. Children negotiated with each other to set parameters of the task as well as with their parents, as shown earlier.

Some parents complained about their children's irresponsibility and their inability to carry out tasks as instructed. Sonia Solis cringed and sat quietly when her mother criticized her for not being capable of carrying out a task. Her eyes filled with tears but they were never quite released. Sonia's mother scolded her because Sonia depended a great deal on other people. For example, she seldom prepared anything for herself to eat, expecting her parents or Marcos to do it for her instead. Mrs. Solis despaired for her daughter's lack of self reliance. Sonia, however, did not see herself in the same way her mother did. She in fact helped out by doing housework and by running errands to Tomás's, although she admitted needing help to run the errands. Sonia also agreed that most of the time she disliked having to do any work around the house and preferred to play with her friends, Marina, Rosa and Maria.

Negotiations began with the acceptance of the task. Children sometimes requested postponement of the task, but generally it was accepted (verbally or nonverbally) immediately. If the details of the task were unclear, children requested clarification either by restating the adult command or by asking a simple question. Children also requested a reward for performing the task. Usually a dime or a quarter was given. Parents gave children spending money if they requested it (twenty-five cents to a dollar) even when a task was not assigned by the adult. Errands to the store often meant spending money for children. At times the request for money compensation became a bargaining tool. Moreover, children negotiated with each other as well as with their parents to set parameters of the task. Occasionally children requested assistance beyond a simple explanation. In response to this request the child received assistance from an adult or another child. Sometimes even if children did not ask for help, other children offered, particularly if when it meant an opportunity to finish the task more quickly. In some cases, though infrequently, children initiated the task in the home. Children, however, more frequently accepted the task assigned by the adults.

Before dinner at the Baca's household, Mrs. Baca asked Adriana to deliver some tortillas to her friend who had called because she was ill and unable to go to the store. Adriana's mother told her that she had to take a dozen tortillas to her friend, Ofelia, because she was not feeling well. Adriana was instructed to tell her that she wished her well soon and that if she needed anything to call Mrs. Baca. Adriana asked her mother if she could take her sister, Mariana. Her mother approved her request but she told her that she had to hurry because they had to return home and help get ready for dinner. Adriana and Marina went on the errand and returned in time to have dinner with the family.

The nature of outdoor tasks were not always errands. Sometimes parents orchestrated tasks that required their children to work collectively to help around the house by caring for the outdoors. The Martinez household, for example, lived in a house with a yard where they kept chickens and other animals.

On one occasion, the father solicited Marina's help by calling for 'mi hijita' (dear). The request for assistance seemed to be a response to a pragmatic need, that is, there was too much trash for Marina to collect by herself. Her father may well have called her by her name because she responded promptly to 'mi hijita'. The entire exchange occurred in Spanish. Since the father wanted the brothers to help, Marina called them for assistance and her father, as the authority, ordered them to help. They completed the task and Marina's father inspected it, approved it, and allowed her to leave. Note that, because it was appropriate to this task, the children were encouraged by the father to work collectively and to take responsibility for completing the task. At other times a task involved two children working simultaneously, but not together.

Mr. Martinez asked Marina to clean up the back yard including the chicken coop. She moaned and said that the boys should also help and she called to Ramon, 'Ven ayudarme' (Come help me). Ramon answered Marina by telling her that he would clean the area where the chickens lived, that was why he had a pail of water. Marina countered by telling that she did not believe him. The three spent a total of a half-hour on the job, with the father occasionally checking to see that the chickens did not leave the fenced area. Marina walked back to the house and put the broom behind the back door. She reported to her father that she had finished and she showed him that she had picked up the papers and trash in the area that she had been assigned.

The collective endeavor to clean the chicken coop was organized by the father. Fighting Marina's and her brother's resistance, the father managed to get them to work together. In the father's absence, the oldest brother assigned tasks to the younger siblings. Marina asserted herself so as not to get stuck with the worse job. In her experience, the person assigning the tasks to younger siblings did the least work. She too had been observed delegating more work to her younger siblings when left in charge. The task, however, was completed with everyone accomplishing his or her respective assignment.

Children also volunteered to do tasks as exemplified by Ramona. Often there were rewards for the children like a trip to their favorite hamburger place. Mrs. Mesa had a bundle of clothes that she was taking downstairs to the wash room. Ramona approached her mother and told her that she wanted to help her wash. Her mother agreed and instructed her to get the box of detergent which was still inside the living room and bring it down to her. When both of them arrived at the laundry room, Mrs. Mesa thanked Ramona, but Ramona insisted on doing more. '¿Que más puedo hacer, mama? Yo quiero poner los quarters en la máquina.' (What else can I do, mom? I want to put the quarters in the machine). Her mother gave her the quarters and Ramona pushed them in the slot. Her mother turned to her and asked her if she wanted to stay near the laundry room to listen for the cycle to be finished. Ramona smiled and nodded her head. When her mother returned to the apartment, Ramona went out by the carport and just swung around the posts and waited for the machine to stop. She found a few twigs and sat on the cement edge of the carport and formed different shapes for several minutes until she heard the ring signaling the machine had stopped, then she ran up the stairs and announced it to her mother.

Ramona's job was complete, but she further insisted on finding out what to do with the clothes. 'Yo sé que tienes que poner la ropa mojada en la secadora, ¿verdad?' (I know that you have to put the wet clothes in the dryer right?) Her mother nodded yes and then asked Ramona to open the dryer door and take the clothes from the washer to the dryer. Again, she asked for permission to insert the coins in the dryer as she had done in the washer. Ramona again said that she would wait for the machine to stop, but this time she told her mother to bring down her roller skates so that she could skate around the sidewalk while she waited. Unfortunately, the machine rang while she was roller skating and she did not hear it. Her mother came downstairs and told her that she needed to be more alert if she was going to be a good helper, 'No puedes estar jugando si vas a ayudarme.' (You can't be playing if you're going to help me.)

What began as a fun activity for Ramona culminated in a strong message to keep play and work separate. Work was serious and when combined with play, one could be negligent as happened to Ramona when she failed to hear the dryer ring because she was skating. The need to be helpful and a part of the family motivated children at times to initiate their role in a chore even without being asked. Children were also well aware of the rewards that were in store for helping around the house.

Children as Interpreters

Literacy activities extended beyond interaction with written text. Bilingual literacy skills were also evident in oral translation exchanges between parents and agents in various institutions. Children became cultural brokers as they attempted to translate and often negotiated with their parents and the agents. Children often help parents by translating at doctors' offices, banks, insurance companies, stores and other businesses where adults had problems understanding. Usually the older children were assigned this responsibility when parents had limited English skills. In some homes there was less need for children to translate if at least one parent had some English skills and was home during the hours when that skill was necessary such as in the Solis household. Mr. Solis had better English skills than Mrs. Solis and he worked the night shift. Therefore, it was easier for him to take care of business that required contact in English with merchants or others. If the case was reversed, however, and the mother had higher English skills than the father, but the father was home during the day because he worked at night, children were called on to help translate when needed.

For example, Marcos went to help his father translate when his baby brother had to be taken to an emergency hospital because he had diarrhea for several days. They waited in the waiting room for forty-five minutes before they were called in. The doctor asked the father, 'Tell me what's been happening?' The father looked at Marcos and Marcos translated, 'Quiere saber qué es lo que está pasando.' (He wants to know what it is that's been happening). The father told Marcos that the baby had diarrhea for four days and that he had a rash on his stomach. They had tried giving him rice water and kept him off milk but that did not seem to help. Marcos turned to the doctor and communicated the response. The doctor continued to examine the baby for a couple of minutes then left the examining area without saying anything. The father turned to Marcos and asked, '¿Ahora a dónde se fue?' (Now where did he go?) Marcos just shrugged his shoulders. He was gone about fifteen minutes before he returned and handed a prescription to the father and told him to give the baby the medication four times a day and the diarrhea should stop within three days because he just probably had a small infection. The doctor left the examining area quickly. Marcos turned to his father and said, 'Que les de la medicina cuatro veces al día y que ya se va aliviar porque no más tiene un poco de infección.' (That you have to give him the medicine four times a day and he'll get well because he just has a small infection.) The father went to the pharmacy and got the prescription there at the hospital pharmacy.

During these translation activities, children's language skills in Spanish and English were solicited as was sociolinguistic knowledge about addressing professional personnel. In the absence of available extended family, parents were sometimes forced to get the older children to help. As important as the service was for the parents, teachers were very concerned about the frequency with which some children were asked to leave school to help the family.

On occasion, children were asked to help out when parents had to deal with businesses, not for translation purposes but for childcare. For example, Mr. Cortes worked days but was able to leave his job for a short time without much problem; his wife could not. He had competent English skills but needed Saul to help him with childcare. One day he had to take his 5-year-old daughter to the doctor and needed Saul to stay with the 2-year-old son. One evening Mr. Cortez announced that he needed Saul to stay home with baby Roberto while he took Olga to the doctor. Saul remembered that he had to turn in some homework in the morning. His father told him that he could turn it in when he arrived at school in the afternoon. Saul knew that the teacher was very strict about returning homework and that if it was not there the first thing in the morning, the student would be penalized. Saul asked his father to take in his homework on his way to the doctor and so that he would not get a bad grade. His father agreed to do it although he did not take kindly to going out of his way.

Saul faced dual loyalty and responsibility in potential conflict. He did not say no to his father's request to help with childcare in the morning, but he did not forget his academic responsibilities. He complied with both his family and teacher expectations by agreeing to stay home with the baby since both parents would be out, and at the same time he figured out a way to honor his classroom commitments.

Although Saul was successful in convincing his father to deliver his homework, some parents did not always understand the importance of complying with school requirements. Mr. Cortez's reluctance about taking Saul's homework to his teacher so that he did not get penalized represented a common attitude on the part of some parents who had not yet learned how to translate their verbal support of education in practice on a day-to-day basis. That is, parents always verbalized a strong belief in education for their children but they did not always know how to operationalize those values. Teachers on the other hand, tended to attribute much of the children's school failure to the perceived parental inability to help their children in matters related to schooling. This included taking children out of school to deal with family responsibilities. This was not the case with Saul who was a high achiever and responsible student. That absenteeism was an educational problem in the schools cannot be ignored. However, the issue of family demands and parental knowledge of school expectations required systematic dialogue between the school and community, including community agencies that could provide services to the family.

Children's interactions with adults and peers in the home revolved around their daily routine which dictated their family life. Children responded to family expectations to cooperate and help each other. In spite of the emphasis for collectivity, children managed many of their activities independently without much parental intervention during the course of the activity. A variety of responsibilities provided the children with contexts in which they learned to be responsible and work collectively by responding to parents' requests and receiving rewards for helping in the organization of the household.

Chores outside of the house varied little from the indoor chores with the exception of the setting. Being outside allowed the children more independence since they did not have their parents as resources once they left the house. As with indoor tasks, children fulfilled their responsibility when sent to the store or on other errands. They completed the task in a reasonable span of time and even negotiated a monetary reward for themselves when trips to the store were involved. Time, trust, responsibility, independence, respect, cognitive skills and a collective spirit all intersected in the variety of household chores in which these children participated.

Summary

How children and adults acted during the household activities made sense to them because of their experience in the work force, their educational background, their socioeconomic conditions, and their perceived needs at any given time. Adults defined roles for themselves and the children in the household activities. While direct, clear, authoritarian patterns of adult behavior surfaced frequently enough in the activities, children also had a great deal of independence in the way that they carried out the task. Parents usually assigned the tasks to the children; they expected the children to be responsible and to assist in the house with family chores. Their notions of interacting with their children were greatly influenced by their own patterns of interaction in what Ogbu, (1981) defines as the cultural ecological domain. Ogbu states that the general and specific skills of human competence lie in the nature of culturally defined adult tasks. In addition, 'certain populations possess unique instrumental competencies that meet their societal needs; and, they adapt their child-bearing techniques to inculcate these needs' (Ogbu 1981:417).

Other researchers (Barry, Child, and Bacon, 1959) claim that the socioeconomic level of adults determines personal attributes and that such attributes seem to influence child-rearing practices. For example, different instrumental competencies are required of adults in two types of society: high accumulation economy and low accumulation economy. Children are likely to be taught the kind of adult behavior useful to the society in which their parents participate (Barry *et al.*, 1959:53–55). While Barry *et al.* examined cultural practices in rural societies, Kohn (1967, 1983) studied American urban society. His findings showed class differences in child-rearing techniques and a relationship to the types of jobs held by the adults. Middle-class professional jobs are associated with personal attributes of self-direction and the ability to manipulate interpersonal relations, ideas, and symbols; working class jobs are associated with respect for authority and conformity to external and imposed rules.

The patterns of interaction between parents and children in these households suggested in this research reveal a complex network of communication. In these families, children exhibited competencies in the use of Spanish, in collectivity, and in respect for authority. Kohn (1983) cautions us against the use of just the family to understand the transmission of values because the children's values are shaped by their experiences in the larger social world. The home, as we have seen, is one setting where children demonstrate their competence largely in response to an authority figure other than themselves; play in the community is one domain where children are the main actors. They select their own settings and activities to a larger degree than in household tasks.

Chapter 4

Storytelling and Games: Learning in Community Settings

Children are active participants in their culture, not merely passive recipients of rules set by adults. In play, children relate to their environment separately from adults, and they create and recreate their own roles. They may literally play out the very rules dictated to them by adults or they may reshape them in concert with their own perceptions when they encounter new situations. In essence, children develop their own view of reality when they interact away from adult supervision. Children's interactions at play integrate the various rules established in the home and in other settings including the classroom. Children's behavior is not as much a function of blind obedience as it may seem. In fact, children may accept, challenge, reverse, comment on, or re-interpret the rules of social order transmitted to them by adults. Play behaviors revealing this complex response are evident in group interaction, between two children or between a single child and an object.

Like household chores, children's leisure activities were affected by the family's socioeconomic status, parental values and children's physical health (Halfon, Jameson, Brindis, Lee, Newacheck, Korenbrot, McCroskey, and Isman, 1989). Children's recreational opportunities in Secoya depended largely on the availability of time, space and imagination. Much of the play in which these children engaged did not require financial resources, not so much because they did not like going skating, swimming or to the movies, but that their parents had made clear the financial constraints that prevented them from paying for children's play activities. The conditions in their neighborhood streets and their public resources become even more important to the families.

Many functions previously performed by the family are now assumed by peer group and community organizations. Children need access to healthy and nurturing areas for play in their neighborhoods. Although children in the Secoya neighborhood did not belong to formal social organizations after school, in the summer they did participate in the Secoya Community Center activities, such as afternoon film series or storytelling hour at the bilingual library.

In his discussions on child development, Vygotsky (1978) concludes that play, although not a predominant feature of childhood, is a leading factor in development (p. 101). In the Secoya community, however, play was the one activity children looked forward to and in which they created and responded to their sociocultural milieu separately from adults. Although children's play routines varied greatly from day to day, the contexts remain fairly constant. Their handclaps, chase games and *cuentos* have endless variations but the settings varied little because of their socioeconomic constraints. Proficient Spanish was the predominant means of verbal communication in play with a few isolated words and phrases in English interspersed during their play events.

Observation of children's play activities revealed that playing a game began either verbally or nonverbally. Sometimes a play activity is begun on a mutual basis, but it may develop into a context which changes the character of the play activity and ends the game. Sitting around or watching television is not considered play. Children characterize their play events by physical movement and a challenge to overcome obstacles, such as other players or objects in the path to an end.

Parents had little comprehension of children's play. They viewed play as a frivolous pastime that consumed too much of children's time and often distracted them from their home chores. Parents reported that their children played a great deal more than they ever did as children in Mexico, where long hours of work in the *ranchos* restricted their play time considerably. Although parents seldom participated in their children's play, they expected their children to play harmoniously. Parents' attitudes about play were colored by their personal experiences and views of the world. Much of the parents' time was consumed by work and the situation was complicated by limited financial resources for recreation.

The families' socioeconomic conditions largely determined where children played. Although Secoya had one small park it was about one-and-a-half miles from their homes. Children were thus confined to areas that were within walking distance or places accessible by bike. Except for Sundays, parents usually could not take the children to a big park out of the area on a regular basis. Furthermore, aside from folk games which they played around the house, other activities required money. Children played in eight general areas: inside their homes, outside their homes, the street, relatives' homes, the railroad tracks, the community park, the school playground and occasionally the swimming pool (when transportation and money were available). Some games were domain specific and could only be played outdoors.

A great deal of variety existed in the amount of time spent playing the different games. In marbles, the boys devote anywhere from ten minutes to a half-hour playing, although one game alone may last from five to ten minutes depending upon the number of players. Card games may go on for an hour if several games are involved, but the players often stay only for one game which may be ten minutes long, after which some players leave and others join. Rarely does the same group play more than two rounds of matching cards.

Bicycle riding seems to engage the boys' attention for a very short period of time, since they circled the block only three or four times before moving on to another activity. Roller-skating may go on for a longer time, but each player's turn is usually about ten times around the circular path that makes up their play area.

Movement-type play consumed much more of the children's time than any other activity. In Secoya, children swing, slide and jump rope as frequently as the equipment is available to them. Both boys and girls aged 3 to 10 years old literally spend hours swinging, sliding and climbing bars when they were on the school playground after school or in the park.

Play was a negotiated activity of interest to the children, an activity in which they adopted negotiable roles or imagined environments. This definition not only encompasses formal games but it also frames informal activities and children's orientation toward an object, person, role, or event so that meaning is derived. Skill play was distinguished from other play not only by its ends but also by the means. That is, in this particular type of play, children needed specific physical skills to achieve their goals.

Children's games can be categorized on the basis of the kinds of actions which determine the outcome. The typology here presumes that the outcome of the game is decided by differences in verbal skill and physical skill. The rules designed by children in their games are congruent with the type of outcome inherent in the game and were modified to meet the children's whims and desires for pleasure. Four major game components include the organization of players, territorial arrangements, game motive and the rules of the game.

To an observer, it seemed that children did little more than play. Whenever they were not in school or doing home chores, they were found engaged in play. From children's perspective, however, there was never enough time for play. The selection of games was never determined by the amount of time they had to play. Every activity had its own life span. Activities became games when children organized a set of rules in which to use their skill.

Storytelling, Verbal Games and Transmission of Knowledge

The children told *cuentos* (stories), played dolls, *casita* (house) and sang chants with each other. Cuentos depended partially on the number of children who wanted to tell a story. Regardless of the number of cuentos, however, the sessions usually lasted no more than fifteen minutes. In the case of dolls and casita, the girls were more likely to play for longer periods than the boys. The boys enjoyed helping the girls build the houses, but as soon as the girls began to assign them roles they became interested in other activities. The length of time spent playing hand-clapping games depends upon the number of chants and/or verses the children knew. The players generally continued until they exhausted their repertoire.

The term 'cuentos' usually has a connotation of cultural folk stories which have been transmitted orally down by the people. Cuentos involved a verbal skill, usually by girls, as a way of engaging friends into a captive audience who would be affected by the plot and outcome of the story. Unlike the challenge of making the mark, as in the swings, in cuentos, children tried to frighten their friends or make them laugh depending on the plot. Children spend many a long afternoon or early evening huddled in small groups on a porch or a small patch of grass somewhere, listening to each other's cuentos. Children sometimes presented their interpretations of popular television characters like Batman woven together with monster characters in the following story told by Mario.

El Monstruo

Había una vez un monstro que era feo pero muy feo. Y el quería comerse a toda la gente no más que la gente eran más fuerte. Y luego una vez el monstruo quería llevarse a un niño y luego batman llegó y agarró al niño y se lo llevó y lo salvó. Se fueron volando los dos y luego [el batman] se lo llevó a sus papas.

Once there was a monster that was ugly, real ugly. He wanted to eat all of the people except that the people were stronger. Then one time the monster wanted to take a little baby and then batman arrived and took the baby and saved him. They both flew off and he [batman] took him to his parents.

Mario developed a story about the characters that impress him the most for their respective strength. In his story, he gave people the attribute of strength but at the end it is a superhuman who saved the day. He abstracted from the immediacy of his present time reality as it appeared on television. Mario's use of 'then' accented the dramatic nature of his story in that he held the children's interest by letting them know that there is more to come. He conveys a sense of despair in the situation but offers a happy ending for the people.

In cuentos, organization takes the form of a story teller and an audience. Although girls usually told the stories, both boys and girls participate as an audience. Many cuentos told by these children were not popularly known: the nature of their stories was local lore picked up by the children from other members of their family or friends. One of the motives of cuentos was also to experience a feeling of danger. The purpose of the activity was to tell the most frightening story, and the children try to top each other's cuento in scariness. Death is one of the most popular themes. Sometimes the scary stories deal with daily events, and caution the children to be careful, like 'El Mudito'. Some of the same scary stories were told at different times by different children but with some of the story changed.

El Mudito

Había un mudito que vivía en una casa y todos los niños le tenían miedo porque también era feo. Y las mamás les decían a los niños que no les hacía nada el mudo que solamente era mudo pero los niños le tenían miedo cuando iban a visitar a la mamá del mudo. Ella no era muda y les contaba cuentos que los asustaban. Pero ese mudito era muy misterioso. Por muchas noches la mamá del mudito estaba dormida y oía que alguien le llamaba y le decía que la iban a matar. Ella no sabía quien era y se levantaba a ver si alguien estaba en la casa pero no veía a nadie. Una noche estaba dormida y otra vez oyo que le llamaba esa voz otra vez. 'Estoy en la cocina y vengo a matarte. Estoy en la sala y vengo a matarte. Vengo a la primera recámara y voy a matarte, Ya estoy aquí en tu cuarto y no te vas escapar.' La mamá estaba bien asustada pero se murió de susto cuando vió que era su el mudito que queria matarla. BOO!

Colorín, colorado este cuento se ha acabado, el que se queda sentado se queda pegado.

There was mute [boy] who lived in a house and all of the children were afraid of him when they went to visit his mother. She was not mute and she used to tell them stories that scared them. But that deaf kid was most mysterious. For many nights his mother heard voices when she slept that told her that she would be killed. She did not know who was calling her [pause and made eye contact with her friends] and she would get up and she did not see anyone. One night she was asleep and again she heard someone calling her, 'I'm in the kitchen and I'm going to kill you. I'm in the living room and I'm going to kill you. I'm in the first bedroom and I'm going to kill you. I'm in your room and you're not going to escape.' [pause and looked around] The mother was horribly scared but she died of terror when she saw that it was her deaf son who wanted to kill her. BOO!

Red color, red color, he who stays seated, stays stuck. (This is an approximate translation to the traditional Spanish saying tagged on to the end of a story. Children were to stand up as quickly as possible when they heard this closure to this story.)

Marina told the story with great dramatic effects, lowering her voice and pausing at right places to further the mystery and capture her friends' attention. The irony was that the children were afraid of the woman's son even though their parents tried to instill in them the need to be tolerant about people who are different from them. However, their sense of something being wrong beyond the person's deafness was highlighted when the person whom they feared the most because he was strange behaved in a way that they did not know how to explain to their parents.

Other cuentos were based on more popular Mexican lore, but the children usually adapted the story by adding bits of real life hearsay. A classic Mexican story is 'la llorona' (the crying woman). Bleich (1988) and Nichols (1989) have addressed the discontinuity in the oral tradition and have concluded that what is transmitted includes more cultural adaptation than actual traditional lore of the story. As the story goes, a woman who was poor and could not feed her children took them to the river and drowned them. The woman felt very lonely and sad so she killed herself. The woman came back as a ghost and is thought to haunt all children who are not good to their parents and to take them to substitute her own. The mention of her is enough to threaten children into behaving properly. The version of 'la llorona' told by these children was not always exactly the same because it was improvised each time they told it.

One early evening a group of children sat around in the front yard of one of the neighbor's house. The story was told by Alicia who had several neighborhood children as her audience, among them Adriana and Mona. Her version went like this:

La Llorona

Una vez había una mujer que estaba loca y no quería a sus niños porque ellos no le ponían atención. Ella los llevó a un río y los mató y luego la señora comenzó a llorar porque ella estaba triste de lo que había hecho y era un pecado mortal porque no debes de matar a gente. Ella se arrepintió y lloró y lloró y nadie le escuchaba, así es que ella se mató y luego se hizo un ghost. Ahora ella anda por todas partes tratando de llevarse niños malos para matarlos como mató a los de ella. Así es que mi mamá siempre nos dice que debemos de obedecerlos porque si no, la llorona puede venir a llevarnos y luego mi mamá se quedarío muy sola.

Once upon a time a lady was crazy and she didn't like her children because they didn't pay attention to her. So she took them to a river and killed them and then the lady began to cry cause she was sorry that she had done it and it was a mortal sin because you're not supposed to kill people. So she felt sorry and then she cried and cried and nobody heard her so she killed herself and then she became a ghost. Now she comes around trying to take bad children and kill them like she killed hers. So my mother always tells me that I should obey them because *la llorona* might come and get me and then mom would be very lonely.

Her friends listened intently and one little boy said that he had seen the llorona once when some cousins took him to a picnic by the river. One girl remarked that he was probably misbehaving and that was why the llorona was around there trying to get him. He defended himself by saying that he was always a good boy.

Filled with suggestions of guilt as a motive, the content of the story reveals some of Alicia's religious training in her plot. Also present were obvious parental threats to discipline Alicia. Regardless, the message of the theme seemed to be integrated so that Alicia and her friends were convinced. The next story had them frowning by the time Rosa's 14-year-old cousin got to the end. She told a story about a family that had four mentally handicapped boys and one beautiful little girl.

La Niña Bonita

Hace muchos años había una pareja que no podía tener niños. Y al fin después de muchos años Dios les dió un hijo. Pero desafortunadamente, el niño nació 'tontito' y no podía pensar muy bien. Pero la pareja lo amaban y dentro poco tiempo tuvieron otro niño. Ese niño también les salió 'tontito'. Pues también a ese niño lo amaban y trataron de enseñarles todo lo possible para que ayudaran en el rancho matando las gallinas y en otro quehacer. El tercer niño también les nació tontito y la pareja dicidieron tener otro niño para haber si les salia un niño normal. No. También el cuarto niño les nació tontito. La pareja les enseñaron cómo hacer el trabajo del rancho y todos los días le ayudaban a la abuela a matar a una gallina, a agarrarla y torcerle el pescuezo. Por algunos años la pareja tenían solo a los niños y un día supieron que la señora iba a tener otro niño. Pues al principio tenían miedo que iba salir igual como los niños pero al fin cuando se alivió la señora se alegraron muchísimo porque les había nacido una niña muy bella. La niña era normal y lindísima. Todos la amaban y la cuidaban como una perla. Los niños jugaban con la niña y la querían muchísimo. Los papas tuvieron que salir un día y dejaron a los niños en la casa cuidando a la niña que ya tenía cinco años y porque la querían tanto y la cuidaban tan bien. Cuando regresaron los padres a la casa, los niños le habían quebrado el pescuezo a la niña.

A long time ago there lived a couple that could not have children. And finally after many years, God gave them a son. But unfortunately, he was born retarded. But the couple loved him and after a short time they had another son. That son was also retarded. Well, they loved that son too and they tried to teach them as much as possible so that they could help around the ranch with killing the chickens. The third child was also born retarded and the couple decided to have another child to see if they would get lucky and have a normal child. The fourth one was also born retarded. The couple taught the boys to do work around the ranch and every day they helped the grandmother to kill a chicken by twisting her neck. For some years the couple had only the boys and one day they learned that the woman would have another baby. At first the couple was afraid that it would be born retarded, but finally when it was born they were thrilled that they had a beautiful little girl. The girl was normal and gorgeous. All of the boys loved her dearly and took care of her and played with her. The parents had to leave one day and left their sons at home to care for their daughter who was now five years old. When the parents returned home, the boys had broken the little girl's neck.

This story shares a similar theme with that of the mute boy who turned out to be evil at the end. The theme of the evil disabled person has, as a basis, fear of what they did not understand and that which was different from themselves.

The rules were more specific for other verbal skill games including 'chants' and 'handclaps.' On the lighter side of verbal play were themes in the handclap chants. In the illustration below the Martinez girls, Mona and Marina, are standing in the front yard of their home after school, handclapping. Mona has a subordinate role in this event.

Marina addressed Mona to tell her that she knew some games. She asked her to put her hands up with palms facing outward. Then, she recited the handclap rhyme while Mona listened.

When Lucy was a baby she used to go like this [Wah! Wah! Wah!] When Lucy was a little girl she used to go like this: 'Hey boy.' When Lucy was a mother she used to go like this: 'Dinner ready.' When Lucy was a grandma she used to go like this: 'I don't know.' When Lucy was a devil, she used to go like this: 'Hey man.'

The girls immediately went on to another verse: 'La Roña' and 'Pepito.' Mona mouthed the words silently to 'La Roña' and 'Pepito' while Marina recited them aloud and confidently. After completing the verse, Marina told Mona that she didn't know any more and her sister also said that she did not know any other. Marina thought for a moment and remembered that she knew 'El Patito' (The Little Duck). Then she said, 'Patito, patito, color de cafe' (Little duck, little duck, of brown color). She tried to recall the rest of the verse but failed to come up with any more phrases and then concluded that she did not know. Mona smiled and said that she did not know any.

Marina initiated the handclapping game with Mona. She knew that Mona did not know as many handclaps as she did. Therefore, the activity was an exhibition of skill. Mona handclapped with Marina and mimicked the rhymes as Marina led. Except for the first rhyme, all the rhymes were in Spanish.

Girls played in these dyads more than boys, although occasionally boys were drawn into dyads to do handclap activity. A handclap game was organized in pairs, with the players facing one another. They clasped their hands, then cross-clap with the partner's hands while rhythmically chanting a verse. If one of the players did not know the verse, the other did the chanting for both.

On a sunny summer afternoon Olga and Mona stood on
the steps of the church waiting for their catechism class to begin.
Mona asked Olga what they should play and Olga answered,
'La Roña' which is a particular chase game. 'La Roña' as other
verbal plays and games demonstrated the versatile rhyme of
children. 'La Roña' is a combination chant and chase activity
where the girls move back and forth and the first one to move
from her frozen position receives a knock on the head. The
rhyme text as well as the girls' directions to each other are in
Spanish. Mona responded that she did not know the game. Olga
invited her to sit down next to her on a small patch of grass and
instructed Mona to stretch out her legs and put her feet against
hers. They held each other's hands and pulled back and forth as
Olga began singing a chant:

> La naranja se murió, el cuchillo la mató, el tenedor y la
> cuchara bailaron rock 'n roll, rock 'n roll. Te apestan los
> pies a carne de res. Te apesta la boca a carne de vaca.
> Uno, dos y tres como caiga usted. El que se mueva
> primero le doy un conscorrón.

> (The orange died, killed by knife. The rock and the
> spoon danced rock 'n roll, rock 'n roll. Your feet smell
> like meat, your mouth smells like cow's meat. One, two,
> three, four as you fall. Whoever moves first gets a nukey
> (knock) on the head.)

Mona began to giggle and Olga reached over to knock her
on the head. Again! Again! On the second round Mona mouthed the words as Olga chanted. Olga giggled first after they
stopped singing and Mona knocked her on the head. Mona got
up quickly and began running away and looked back to see if
Olga was following her. Olga chased Mona.

Vygotsky (1978) states that play is not very original imag-
ery because imaginary situations are usually reproductions of
real situations. Children reproduce real life experiences but they
also adapt the schema by creating their own version of the
outcomes. Simulation play combined different typology such as
skill, strategy and luck. In simulation play children imagine a

situation and break away from the constraints of organized play where rules governed their games. Griffin (1984) concludes that if we consider children as cultural members, play brings their social abilities into perspective. She states that if children are capable of communicating symbolic meanings and know it, and interact as though the symbols were real, such involvement indicates an evolved form of communication. Mead, much earlier, in 1967, believed that role-taking as it occurs in symbolic play was a step toward social maturity. Bateson (1972) also believed that children develop communication skills in role playing because of its metaphoric nature and viewed it as a step in human communication. In Secoya, simulation play was a form of symbolic play and simultaneously real for children. The girls assumed the position of 'mommy' and their dolls became the 'babies'. Where did skill, strategy and luck come into the picture when playing house? Casitas, playing house, was played outside, usually near the garbage cans behind the apartment building or in back yards. Casitas was also played by both girls and boys, with the players took turns as mommy, daddy, and babies. Boys picked up cardboard boxes from the railroad area two blocks from most of the children's houses. The boxes became walls and roofs for the doll houses. The boys helped the girls set up the simulated houses to play dolls. An interesting point was that almost all of the fathers in these families had some role in childcare. Yet in these children's organization of casita the boys usually did not involve themselves with dolls. They only helped to set up the play areas.

Dolls were played either indoors or outside. Mona, for example, often played indoors where she built an elaborate house for her doll in her bedroom, using pillows and old clothes. She hung clean clothes from a basket on hangers and on a wire around a stack of pillows where she placed her dolls. Alicia talked to her dolls as if they were real babies, 'Ya sé que quieres una botella con leche. Mira aquí la tengo'. (I know you want a bottle with milk. Look here it is.) She put a popsicle stick in one doll's mouth and then placed the other two dolls facing each other as she made up conversation with between the dolls. One doll was given this line: 'Quiero que vayas a la tienda porque necesito unas tortillas.' (I want you to go to the store because I need tortillas.) 'Sí mamá yo voy y me compro un dulce también.' (Yes mom I'll go and buy myself a candy too.) For a couple of minutes, Alicia completed the scenario for her dolls to go to the store.

In the absence of play equipment like bottles and beds for her dolls, Mona improvised and provided for her dolls everything from comfortable surroundings to words and specific chores. The dialogue assigned to the doll, including references to chores, reflected that which Mona hears and sees around her even though she herself was not yet responsible for many household chores.

Simulating real events was fairly typical when children played with dolls whether alone or with others. But not all simulation play was a replay of their real experience. Children also pretended when they played with dolls, toy cars, or other equipment which they designed. Sometimes they found objects lying on the streets around which they spontaneously organized an adventure.

One late afternoon, for example, three boys and two girls were returning from a trip to the store and Mario picked up a long narrow stick. Marcos took the salt which he had bought to his mother and returned to play with his friends. By then, Mario had tried to shape the end of the long narrow stick into a sharp point by beating the end of the stick on the cement sidewalk. Adriana had run inside her house to get two scarves and came back outside to the group who had situated themselves next to a short wooden fence by a small apartment complex. Mario told the boys that they were his helpers who were trying to help him fight the monster and he was the king who was going to kill the monster. Adriana assigned her and Ramona the role of fairy princesses who were going to save all of the people in the town from the monster. They wrapped their scarfs around their shoulders and ran up and down the sidewalk. Mario got on top of the short fence and started pointing at the boys. Marcos decided that he would be the monster and scare them all. Mario ran back and forth on the top of the fence and the girls yelled out, '¡Nosotros los salvamos! !Nosotros los salvamos!' (We'll save you! We'll save you!) Mario and his friend meanwhile waved his stick and told the monster that he would die soon because his weapon was sharp and dangerous. As Mario pretended to eliminate the monster, the girls ran inside Ramona's house shouting, '¡Ganamos, Ganamos!' (We won! We won!)

Apparently the people won against the monster. The boys and girls had assumed roles to collectively wage a struggle against their imagined monster. In their imaginary event, children subordinated their objects as they attributed real meaning to them. Vygotsky comments on an imaginary situation by saying that it is children's first manifestation of emancipation from situational constraints (Vygotsky, 1978). Children retained the properties of the stick and the scarfs and fence but changed their meaning as Alicia did with the popsicle sticks when playing with her dolls.

Games of Strategy and Physical Skill

Riding a bike, swimming, running in chase games, and distance jumping were only a few activities in this category. Cards also were popular with both boys and girls. Whether two or eight children gathered, cards were objects by which children played out important cognitive skill in concentration.

A group of children congregated outside of the Mesa home. It included Ramona, her older sister, Tomás and Mario and Sonia Solis. Marcos called to play the cards which he brought with him. Without any inquiry from the children, he automatically began to shuffle all the cards and then turned them all face down. Marcos said 'Yo primero' (I'm first). Others followed suit and called out numbers for the positions. The one who called out loudest got the next number, and so on. Ramona's sister was second, Ramona third, Sonia fourth and Tomás fifth. The group sat around in a circle and Marcos picked up one card, thought for a few seconds then exclaimed 'Oh, no!' (shucks) when he realized that they did not match. Ramona's sister picked up Marcos's second and also failed to get a match. Ramona, however, got a match. Sonia and Tomás followed with no success. This prompted a comment from Marcos: 'A ver si esta vez consigo un par. No más Cecilia tiene uno.' (Let's see if this time, I get a pair. Only Cecilia has one.)

The second round was more successful for all except for Tomás. After the first round, he still had none. Cecilia then had two pairs. The third round meant even more success for Marcos and Cecilia. When Ramona had her turn, she now had three pairs and handed one over to Tomás and told him, 'Tomás, yo tengo, a ver si así tienes buena suerte'. (Here, I already have one and maybe this will be good luck.) Tomás accepted the pair without a word. He took his turn as usual and smiled broadly when he found his first matching pair.

Almost thirty minutes later, the third round of the card game began and almost everyone was able to get a matched pair. Everyone kept a count of the pairs they had and reminded the group what they had. 'Yo tengo tres pares.' 'Yo tengo dos pares.' 'Yo tres.' 'Yo también.' (I have three pairs. I have two pairs. I have three. Me too.) Although they kept close check on the individual gains, the challenge seemed to be more in comparing what they gained each at each turn. The idea of competing with each other was not apparent until the last round when most of the cards were played. Children sat with their individual stack of cards and Marcos had the most and called out, 'Gane, tengo mas.' (I won, I have more.) 'Yo también tengo cinco.' (I have five too), called Cecilia. 'Ok', said Ramona, 'Los dos ganaron y luego yo y luego Sonia y luego Tomas.' (you both won and then me and then Sonia and then Tomás.) The game was over.

The object of matching cards, a favorite and typical card game, to collect the most pairs by the end. The game finished when all the cards have been picked, and the player with the most cards had the first turn in the next game. Ordinarily, this type of game can be construed as competitive, as the players either win or lose, but these children sometimes modified the rules so that players who had more pairs voluntarily gave some of their pairs to others with fewer cards. Another variation of the rules occurred at the end of the game; ordinarily, there is only one winner by ranking the players according to the number of pairs acquired in the game. Rather than have one person be the 'winner', the players cooperated by sharing their matched pairs with those with fewer pairs.

The game shows how the children compete with each other in English for their respective turns in the game. Initially Marcos called out the loudest and he was first. Most of the children's interactions were in Spanish with isolated single words and short phrases in English indicating position in the game. The closure of the game showed that one's victory is victory for all. All of the players were relegated a winner's position: first, second, third, fourth. This showed collective behavior within a traditionally competitive context.

Chase

Chase games were also played outdoors, where there is sufficient space for the players to chase one another. Chase games were played by boys and girls, although more often than not the participants were girls. These children's versions of the traditional Mexican folk games, 'Blanca Nieves' (Snow White); and 'La Vieja Inéz' (Old Lady Inéz), involved pursuit of one or several of the players. In the first, the players confined their play to a circle, while 'La Vieja Inéz' required more extended activity.

'La Vieja Inéz' is a popular chase game among the children. In this game, the key role was the Vieja Inéz who announced herself. If a boy played the role, he changed it to the male form, El Viejo Inez. The vieja initiated the game by saying 'knock, knock.' The 'mother' is the lead role for the group opposing the vieja. She whispered a color in the ear of each player in her team. The 'mother' responded to the vieja's knocks by asking who is it to which the vieja responded, 'La Vieja Inéz.' The mother then asked the vieja what she wanted. The vieja said that she wanted a ribbon. The mother asks what color specifically and the vieja gave a color. The person assigned the specific color called upon by the vieja is then pursued by La Vieja Inéz. If caught, that person became the vieja's captive. The game ended when the Vieja Inéz captured the mother. This game is adapted according to the number of players or when conditions changed due to colder wet weather outside, children having to assume childcare responsibilities indoors, children being punished by staying indoors or when they were ill and unable to go outside.

One instance where different conditions forced the children to adapt this game happened when it was cold outside and Saul's brother Roberto was ill. Saul had to take care of him while his parents went to get a prescription for him. Friends came to join them in their house. All six children crowded into the bedroom. First, the children lay on the floor and glanced through two large family photo albums, then Antonia, Saul's neighbor, suggested that they play Vieja Inéz. The children looked around the room momentarily without comment then Rosa jumped up and said that she knew how to they could play Vieja Inéz without having to run. Antonia said that Rosa could be the Vieja Inéz and she would sit in on floor on one side of the room while everyone else who was going to be a color to get on the other side of the room. Olga assigned herself the 'mother' role and Antonia suggested that she begin to give each team member a color but emphasized that she had to whisper so Rosa would not hear. Antonia continued instructing everyone to get started and Olga began to whisper colors to her team members. Rosa said, 'Knock, knock.' Olga asked 'Quien es?' (Who is it?) She said, 'the Vieja Inéz.' When they got to the color, Rosa asked for the color yellow. Antonia suggested that the person whose color was guessed should go sit on the larger bed. Mario who was the color yellow got up and went to sit on the bed. Rosa clapped her hands and said, 'You're out! You're out!' a feature of the game not seen when children play outside and are able to chase each other.

During the second round of the game, the color red was called and again the vieja guessed correctly. The person who was the color red went to sit on the bed. Marcos was the last color to be guessed and he automatically became the 'Viejo Inéz.' Antonia assigned herself the 'mother's' role and she gave everyone in her team a color. Rosa then began to play the leader's role which Antonia had in the first part of the game. She told Marcos to get the game started. He knocked on the door and announced himself, 'El Viejo Inéz'. Antonia asked him what he wanted and he said a color. She asked what color. Marcos responded, 'Pink.' 'Pink?' yelled Antonia. '!Tu eres un tramposo! Tu oiste.' (You cheater! You heard.) She insisted that they do it over and removed Marcos from the position and made Maria the Vieja Inéz. Antonia gave Marcos the 'mother' position. Maria began the game by knocking and asking for the color blue. Antonia told her that it was not any of the eight colors, and Antonia assured her that she would never guess the colors because they were all muted pastels. Marcos, in his 'mother' role kept asking Maria what color she wanted. Maria said, 'Gray.' Antonia told her that it was almost like a grey; her clue to Maria was, 'Es compañero del grey.' (It's a partner to gray.) Maria was persistent and continued knocking and asking for other colors without any success. The children began to get restless and seemed to lose interest. For example, Rosa left because her mother called her. Maria also left because she said she wanted to do something else and Mario just announced that he did not want to play any more. The game they played for nearly an hour ended due to lack of interest or maybe because Antonia made it too hard.

Antonia, the oldest in the group, initiated the game. The rest had a vague recognition of the rules, which gave Antonia an advantage over the others, but she did not teach them until Olga and Rosa learned the process. Once they became familiar with the process, they begin to cue other players. In this game, the children labeled their colors in English and called out rules like 'You are out.' But most of their play interaction and the text occurred in Spanish. Antonia used most of the English phrases. Her English-speaking proficiency was more advanced than the others'. Although Antonia initiated the game, she allowed Rosa, Olga and Marcos to assume the power roles (Vieja Inéz and la mamá). Power roles were alternated among the children. Sometimes the roles were claimed voluntarily and a couple of times the positions changed as part of the expected sequence of the game. There was no culmination of winners and losers in this game. The game proceeded for a few rounds and the game ended when the Segura sisters were called out by the parents. In this game, Marcos was caught cheating when he tried to overhear the color.

Chase games were among the more popular skill games. Movement games were generally played on the school playground or in the neighborhood parks, where swings, slides and climbing bars provided the activities for the various types of movement play which the children enjoy. Bicycle riding and roller-skating were also played outdoors, but generally closer to home than movement games. The boy's territory for bike-riding was around the block or down the driveway, while roller-skating usually took place in the carport area of the apartment building, around parked cars.

In group chase games, children called out for their turns in the card game, taking turns as dictated by the game structure. In some of the chase games, children adapted traditional titles of the Mexican game. For example, 'Doña Blanca', was renamed 'Blanca Nieves'. The adaptation incorporated the children's knowledge of the Walt Disney version of the Grimm fairy tale character which they had seen on television and read about in storybooks. Except for the name substitution, the game remained the same. The game was organized in a similar pattern to the other two, this time beginning with a dialogue between the chaser and all the other players. At the end of the dialogue, the chased broke through the circle and the pursuit ensued until s/he was caught or returned safely to the circle. If caught the person returned to the circle and the pursuer went in the middle of the circle. The more capable runners made it back to the circle without being caught, in which case Blanca Nieves had a choice of returning to the center of the circle or choosing someone go into the circle. The children's lyrics to the song Blanca Nieves were adapted from the traditional version. Their song lyrics were:

Blanca Nieves está cubierta con pilares de oro y plata. Romperemos un pilar para jugar con Blanca Nieves.

(Snow White is protected behind columns made of gold and silver. We're going to try and break a column to play with Snow White.)

The traditional lyrics to the song were:

> Doña Blanca está cubierta con pilares de oro y plata. Romperemos un pilar para jugar con Doña Blanca. ¿Quién es ese jicotillo que anda rodeando mi casa? Yo soy ese, yo soy ese, que anda en pos de Doña Blanca.

> (Mrs. White is protected behind gold and silver pillars. We're going to try and break a column to play with Mrs. White. Who is that suitor who lurks around my house? I am he. I am he who is in pursuit of Mrs. White.)

All the circle games have an unlimited number of players. Organization of the participants was kept fairly simple, with only two main actors and a circle of players. There was an automatic rotation of players established by the players' ability to run and or their choice of whom they chose to pursue them. In the game 'Naranja Dulce' (Sweet Orange), for example, the child circling the outside circle has a handkerchief which he/she drops behind the person they choose to pursue them. Children sing the song as they circle around holding hands, but the song stops when the chase begins. The song lyrics to Naranja Dulce are:

> Naranja dulce limón partido dame un abrazo que yo te pido. Si fueran falsos mis juramientos en otros tiempos se olvidaran. Toca la marcha mi pecho llora, adiós señora yo ya me voy.

The version which the children sang differed from the traditional one. Their version of Naraja Dulce was:

> Naranja dulce limón partido dame un abrazo que yo te pido. Si fuera rico yo te daría unos listones de (hum hum hum). Adiós muchachos yo ya me voy para Felicia de donde yo soy.

> (Sweet orange and sliced lemon give me a hug that I ask of you. If I have deceived you you'll forget it in time. Let

the band play, my heart hurts. Good bye my dear, I am now leaving.)

Other chase games included 'Las Escondidas' (Hide and Seek), with the person designated as 'It', looking for the 'hiders'. Various versions of 'tag' were played in the swimming pool or on the monkey bars.

Some games allowed children to rotate turns with less pressure for an individual goal. The following example is a Mexican folk game where the rules are relaxed to adapt the game to a different setting. The interaction captures a sense of the informal teaching and learning routine in a collective setting.

After church one Sunday at St. Joseph's, Ramona, Sonia and Olga got out of the children's religious class and waited for their parents to come out of church. They began a chase game when Sonia called out, '¿A ver quién la tiene?' (Let's see who is it?) They determined who was 'it' by doing a counting game: 'De pin marin de do pin guey, títara mácara títere fué. Quién fué yo no fuí, pégale, pégale que ella fué.' The rhyme does not translate in any way that would make sense. The nonsensical rhyme identifies a person by pointing to them systematically until the end of the verse. 'Un pie, no los dos.' (One foot, not two.) The three girls extended one foot in as they faced each other and Sonia pointed at the girls feet as she recited the rhyme. Olga called out to Ramona, 'Cuenta despacio.' (Count slowly). Their pre-game ceremony identified Ramona to be 'it', the pursuer, while the other two girls ran to hide behind the church building.

Ramona called out to the girls: 'Uno, dos, tres ... veinte. Alli voy.' (One, two, ... twenty. I'm coming.) She ran to look for the girls. Ramona found Olga first and ran to try and tap home base first before Olga. Ramona outran Olga and told her that now she was 'it.' Ramona called out to Sonia and told her that Olga was 'it' now because she was found first and she had not touched home base. Sonia asked the girls, '?Ok, ahora quién le toca?' (Ok, who's turn is it?) Olga said, '?Yo, que no oyes, sorda?' (I am, didn't you hear, are you deaf?) Olga turned away from the girls with her head against the wall and began to count. The girls ran to hide, but before Olga had finished counting to twenty, Ramona came running from around the corner and announced that her older sister was calling her so she had to leave. Olga stopped counting and waited for Sonia to come back.

Although initially, 'it' was selected through a pre-game rhyme, children had an automatic turn to be 'it' for subsequent rounds of the game as the game unfolded. Various forms of sharing equally were practiced. Spanish was spoken exclusively in the sparse verbal interaction. Their game was interrupted by the family's need to get the girls home. A consistent sequence of turns characterized the game which was motivated by their intent to outrun each other and get to safety before the pursuer. While children did not play 'escondidas' to establish winners and losers they nevertheless reveled in finding a perfect hiding place and outrunning each other.

In 'brincado los columpios' (jumping the swings), a name that clearly describes the game, children took turns swinging high and jumping off. One summer afternoon five children, Mona, Sonia, and Raul, Jesus and Marcos walked to the park which was near the more industrial part of town. The boys played on the swings while the girls did somersaults on the small grass area part of the park. Upon arriving, the boys ran to the swings and swung back and forth for a couple of minutes. Marcos jumped off the swing and returned to his swing. Raul jumped off next and noticed where he landed then challenged his friends to beat his jump. After jumping off he then told Mario to jump off and notice how far he jumped. Mario jumped as the other two boys were back on their swings. He was impressed with how far he had jumped and asked his friend to notice. Raul jumped again and said he had not jumped as far as the last time. He marked the spot where he landed with a stick and then told his friends to watch him cause he was going to exceed the mark. He jumped and landed beyond his mark. The boys cheered him and said they were going to jump farther than their previous mark, 'Yeah! yo voy a brincar más allá del mio también, 'ira.' (Yeah! I'm going to jump farther than my mark too, watch.) Marcos jumped and said his jump was good and then made an 'X' on the dirt. On his next jump he fell short of his mark and in a disappointed tone, he promised his friends that he would beat his mark. Mario went a step farther and said that he could jump to where a part of a branch was lying. He jumped and came within an inch of his goal. He became excited that he had jumped quite a distance. Mario jumped off the swing and ran to another area of the park. Raul called to him and then decided to join him. Marcos sat at the swing for a few short minutes than joined the others.

Children's play did not always have defined group organization. Their interaction with each other and with their environment, however, makes a telling point about what is important to the children. A simple swing brings challenge as the boys try to beat their own mark. The boys seemed to notice only their own jumps and tried to match them against their previous try rather than comparing their distances against the other two boys'. Although the jump game began somewhat competitively when Raul invited the boys to jump farther than he had, none of the boys made a claim to victory at the end.

Bicycles were also ridden primarily by boys, who doubled up on one bike to ride around the block. If one boy was ahead, he determined an imaginary boundary, rode up to it, and then waited for his friend to catch up to him. Roller-skating was an activity for both boys and girls, who skate in pairs and or alone.

Marbles

If one type of game demands that children act against their immediate impulse of spontaneity, it is a game of strategy. Strategy games required children to use mental operations to plan a way of accomplishing their goal. The Secoya children organized themselves in a variety of ways, depending upon the type of outcome of the particular game being played. Girls participated more in verbal games than did boys. In activities involving toy cars and marbles, boys participated, but girls were excluded.

Marbles games were played either in pairs or alone. They involved turn-taking, with careful attention paid to which marble should be hit so that a point will be scored. As the player scored a point he won his opponent's marble. Marbles are likely to be played on a paved area near a building, so that the players could shoot their marbles at the wall. In the absence of a wall, the boys draw an arbitrary line as a boundary. The game of marbles tends to be more competitive than other games. The rules are to have the marble hit as many marbles as possible as it goes through the *cuadrito* or the *círculo* without ending inside. The player is 'out' if his marble gets stuck. The winner gets the loser's marble and they continue playing to try and win it back.

One of the most frequently played games was called *Choya* (Crow). There were usually four boys participating. A circle was drawn around a shallow dip in a dirt area. A second circle was drawn to mark off the area from where the boys were to shoot. Each player stakes out their own space inside the innermost circle and tries to knock another player's marble out of the circle. If a player hits another's marble out of the circle, he gets to keep the marble. The player with the most marbles wins.

In marbles boys did not share their winning with each other as they appeared to at the end of the card games. Possibly it was because the boys who carried around a large bag of marbles had status over those who had few or none.

Although boys tried to keep girls from interfering with their games, girls did their best to bother the boys so that they could not exclude them entirely. Becoming part of the boys' team on those occasions never seemed to be as important as interrupting the game.

The Social Context of Play

In play, the Secoya children formulated their own rules for interacting. Children in the 7 to 10 year age group were old enough to play unsupervised; they usually sought out other children, and rarely played alone. When invited to play, friends usually accepted, although the child initiating might not specify a game when making the invitation. Thus, even the type of game is often negotiable. When an invitation to play was declined, it was usually because a child's parents had made other plans for him or her. As a general rule, children who wished to play were free to invite a friend or sibling to participate, regardless of their ages.

Children's verbal and nonverbal ways of organizing themselves in play events were illustrated. Children spoke in Spanish with each other for imperatives, hints, expressions and clarifications in challenging each other. Much of the game text in their rhymes and verses was recited in Spanish, with only a few game texts recited in English.

Children established patterns of interaction as they observed and changed the rules in their play. Both younger and older children assumed responsibility for initiating play activity as they sought out friends and siblings. Sometimes children challenged each other competitively, but more frequently they hinted at inviting or directly invited one another to play. Their interactions with each other revealed relationships of players to one another and the multiple roles of each player. As they negotiated rules, created new ones, agreed to variations and denounced a 'cheater' in the Vieja Inéz game, children explored relationships. They learned about the value of power, personality, and respect for each other.

The norms of conduct in children's play formed activities for interaction, such as playing in mixed groups, taking equal turns, and joining forces against an antagonist, symbolizing collective and egalitarian practices. Power roles in children's play activities indicated status within the play group. Every play event offered an opportunity for children to demonstrate their leadership and ability to follow. The only consistent rule in reference to power roles in the play group studied was that leadership positions should be alternated. Occasionally the group divided across gender lines but seldom divided by age. In a mixed group, the children played interchangeable roles. Sometimes personality constituted a factor in status assignments. For example, Mona, who was rather shy, assumed a follower role when playing with Rosa, Marcos and Marina, but when playing with Sonia she asserted herself in a leadership position since Sonia was also a sensitive person. As a result, Mona, although one of the younger players in this cohort, participated in diverse roles in play. These children also manifested more collective tendencies than competitive practices in their games. However, we cannot conclusively state that Secoya community children were entrenched in only one form of behavior since some of their play attempts to mesh the two forms of collective and competitive cultural patterning.

Summary

Children maximized their available resources (space and play events) creatively. The play types — skill, chase, swinging, cuentos and simulation — were organized by rules according the outcomes of games such as marbles, jump rope, casita or Las Escondidas. Rules, space and time of a game were negotiated among the children.

Children designed their own rules for interaction in play, rules which often reflected their home tasks. For example, collective behavior, a common practice in household activities was characteristic of play events. The language of interaction in play was the same as that of the home, but more English was heard among the children at play with peers than at home with adults. In play activities, children experimented with English among peers. During the course of the study children used more English in their play when asking questions about rules of the game indicating that rules in the use of language are contextual and flexible. Although children engaged in play without others, for the most part, an egalitarian ethic in turn-taking in group interaction was observed both in the home and play. However, parental authoritarian practices over children often characterized games about home chores.

Children's collective and egalitarian practices in play organization are socially negotiated activities. Enactment of games is one of the variables compared in Fisher and Fisher's (1963) research of six cultures. The study showed that Anglo children often compete in social interactions, while all other cultures, including Spanish-speaking children in the United States, approach their play activities less competitively.

Chapter 5

From School to Home

Classroom activities differ from those in the informal settings. School rules and policies govern classroom instruction, making its nature inherently formal. The work of Cole (1985), Cole and D'Andrade (1982) and Diaz, Moll and Mehan (1986) as well as Tharp and Gallimore (1989) has illustrated that the classroom setting provides a context in which children integrate culture, cognition and skills. The seven classrooms observed had many similarities, in spite of the fact that they operated in different schools in the same community. The commonalities were in the three major structures which constituted instruction, large group teacher-directed activities, and small group activities and independent tasks.

Children liked school because their friends were there and because they generally liked their teachers. Except for Raul and occasionally Jesus, the other twelve children attended school regularly. Their interest in being at school was related to their perceived success in the classroom. They felt that they were learning and liked the work that they did in class, regardless of the objective reality of the situation. Raul and Jesus were two exceptions. Due to their frequent absences, these students were usually lost when they did attend and could not follow the classroom routine, thus increasing their sense of failure. Although the students were at different levels of achievement, they all believed that they were learning. The classroom activities in which these children participated revealed the extent to which children used the skills learned outside of the classroom and their ability to adapt to the different expectations of the classroom.

Classroom activities were governed by a conscious set of rules. The way in which children related to each other, to their teacher and to the work showed their native culture in action. Those same behaviors revealed the extent to which children had learned to operate within the cultural dictates of the classroom, which might or might not be like those the children had learned in their home and community. This was determined by the way that the learning activities were designed by the teacher.

Social and cultural rules for interaction in classroom learning activities meant more than a list of dos and don'ts displayed on the chalkboard. The rules were designed by the teachers who also designed their learning activities for math, reading and all other subject areas. Their beliefs, values and ideology were transmitted to students via the activities in which children participated. Leacock (1969) and Apple (1979) have concluded that the teachers' decisions are influenced by social considerations. Spindler (1963:156) has also informed us of the way in which teachers, while they may be the instrument for transmitting culture in the classroom, are not solely responsible for the values imparted. The teacher is carefully trained to fulfill the role of official cultural transmitter. The professional institutions are organized according to certain values and symbols and beliefs. The cycle repeats itself as teachers begin their training in the elementary school to which they later return to teach (Leacock 1969:148). During their careers in these institutions they learn to adapt to the culture of the particular school in which they teach.

Cultural values are also transmitted by the language a teacher uses to conduct class. Some teachers use more English than Spanish in the classroom, even when the children's dominant language is Spanish; the reason given for this practice is that Spanish-speaking children should learn English quickly to ensure their success in school. Someone making this argument clearly does not know the principle of bilingual instruction. Such claims also point to the teacher's belief that English is a more vital vehicle for instruction and 'success' language status is a culturally-learned value.

Schools are expected to train children socially and

academically; children's careers in the school consisted of lesson upon lesson intended to edify them. These classroom lessons are framed by cultural codes. For example, reading is taught in most societies, but how, where, when and what one reads are determined by the culture in which one participates. Social rules of behavior related to the task of reading are culturally bound, and schools are established to transmit those accepted norms of conduct related to the learning of any academic subject in accordance with the belief of the dominant culture (Leacock, 1969; Spindler 1974). Therefore, the teacher's part and the student's role in the instructional process are guided by broader cultural norms that ensure that the learner will conform to the behaviors required by the dominant culture.

Teaching Spanish-Speaking Children

Two of the seven teachers observed were native bilingual speakers. While the other teachers were Anglo, they were bilingual with varying degrees of Spanish proficiency. The teachers generally designed their own version of a bilingual program according to what was learned in workshops and meetings. While the district had general guidelines, the teachers met only occasionally to receive the latest information about bilingual instruction and to share ideas. When possible, some teachers visited other bilingual classes outside the district and attended conferences to acquaint themselves with new methods and curricula for bilingual children.

Generally, teachers in the first grades used more Spanish than did teachers in the second and third grades. The use of Spanish diminished in the formal curriculum as children progressed in grades. This was due to the belief that children should have acquired sufficient English to be able to transfer to the all-English curriculum by the fourth grade. A number of assumptions were made here. First, it was assumed that all children learned a second language at the same pace. Second, it was assumed that all children entered the school at a kindergarten level and they had the same level of language development in Spanish when they began school. Third, it was assumed that because children were bilingual at a verbal level they could fully comprehend the textbook curriculum in English.

Each teacher had his/her own unique way of dealing with children. Some believed that Spanish-speaking children had to be taught in Spanish so that they could learn English as soon as possible. For the most part they were concerned that the children came from low income families who could not provide them with the necessary skills before coming to school, and, therefore, they as teachers had to work harder to teach the children so that they could eventually be on par with their Anglo mainstream counterparts. Teachers felt committed to working with Spanish-speaking children because they believed that children needed extra academic attention and they were willing to provide it.

Children's activities outside of the classroom lend insights about their sociocultural and cognitive development in natural settings. Classroom activities help to further explain children's adjustment to school as they attempt to make sense of their home culture in the school context. Questions remain as to what is learned in school and how children manifest their feelings and their knowledge when they take the school home. The purpose of this chapter is to analyze the classroom activities from the children's and teachers' point of view in an attempt to understand how children were socialized to school and what aspects of school were taken home.

From the Children's Viewpoint

Rewards and consequences were relatively clear in all of the classrooms. When children followed the rules set forth by the teacher they were rewarded usually with verbal recognition. The class rules generally asked students to arrive to school on time, work quietly, not to chew gum or eat in class, not to talk while the teacher was talking, and to be courteous to others in class. Teachers used verbal rewards to get students to quiet down when they wanted their attention. Usually, there was no problem in getting children to quiet down. With the exception of one or two children in the classroom who were considered by the teachers to be 'discipline problems', they wanted to please the teacher. It was not the case that the 'problem' children did not want to please the teacher, rather they were not convinced that what they were doing was wrong and found themselves in situations where they could not comply with the rule. The rules in the setting, however, applied to all and teachers were adamant that all children should respect them. A second grade teacher expressed sentiments common to the rest of the teachers when she said, 'Children are given a rule, then they have a choice to follow it or not. They know the consequences each time they do not follow the rules. They also get a reward certificate when they obey.' This was not the way children viewed the rules. They seemed to feel that there were always circumstances that should be considered. For example, when they came in late from recess, they thought the teacher should accept their excuse that there were too many children in line at the drinking fountain and that was what delayed them. Teachers, of course, wanted their side understood, that class began for all at the same time and that they did not want to explain directions more than once to accommodate the tardy students. While most children had no problem remembering to get to class on time or not to chew gum in class or not talk while the teacher was talking, children like Jesus, for example, consistently fond themselves in conflicting situations with the teacher or peers.

Jesus, a first grader at Gardner school, liked to talk and had difficulty deciphering when it was appropriate and when it was not. He often talked to those around him about everything from his fall on the playground to his mother's trip to the doctor. When the teacher caught him talking, she put his name on the board and for each additional infraction he got a check next to his name. The first check meant that the student would have to stay in for one recess, the second check meant staying after school, the third check meant a call to the parent, and a fourth check meant the principal's office. In Jesus' case as with other students who were considered 'problems', his name appeared on the board constantly. On some days, Jesus found himself spending more time inside than outside during recess. Although demoralized by not being able to play with his classmates at recess, he pursued conversations with them during class, which per-petuated the cycle of constant conflict and punishment for breaking the rule. Jesus was ridiculed by his peers for always being in trouble. This criticism for talking too much in class may have been responsible for Jesus' chronic absenteeism.

Jesus seemed to like school when questioned. He responded enthusiastically about the things he liked, math and physical education. His attendance pattern, however, indicated a real neglect of school. His mother said that he did have lots of colds, especially in the winter, but apparently sometimes Jesus had been known to be absent when his mother said she had sent him to school.

Breaking classroom rules was very common for children in other classrooms. Raul, a repeat second grader in Oakgrove school, was very familiar with breaking one of the most impor-tant rules: 'get to school on time'. The consequence of his infraction was that Raul missed recess when he arrived late, which occurred frequently. Raul had had a similar problem in his second grade classroom the previous year, (Delgado-Gaitan, 1983) which was the reason he was retained in the same grade. The nature of his absenteeism differed from Jesus' in that Raul usually stayed out of school because he was playing without his parents' knowledge or permission. The cycle of Raul's loss of interest in school, his response to the classroom rules, and his school performance was indeed symbiotic. The reality for Raul, as he expressed it, was anger about not being able to participate in school as a result of the rules and consequences. His inability to get to class on time in the mornings consistently set him up for conflict with the teacher. When he attended school and arrived late, he began the day with his name on the board and a check next to it. He automatically lost his first recess. Another way in which absences affected his class performance was that he seemed confused about the classroom routine and inevitably talked out of turn or was caught walking around the room, which was against the rules. The teacher seemed to understand that Raul had problems conforming to the classroom rules; however, she felt that she had to be tough with him because, 'If you let them get away with stuff at this young age, they'll never learn how to get along in school.' Raul felt as did Jesus that they did not do anything wrong and disliked being singled out for staying in during recess. They believed that it was not fair that they could not play with their friends and that other kids laughed at them for being caught.

The teachers distinguished between those students who they claimed tried hard and those that just wanted to bother others. Teachers believed that it was not fair for students who were not serious about learning to come to class and disrupt the regular routine. They held the truant students responsible for their behavior and felt justified in imposing the same rules on the truants and the rest of the students. Some of them believed that staying in with the teacher at recess might be a treat more than a punishment because the students got special attention from the teacher. They nevertheless continued the practice of holding students in during class. In some cases many students were held in across several classes; when teachers wanted to take a break they just sent their students to a designated teacher.

Children's Socialization in the Classroom

Classroom events represent a framework for understanding how the activities are constituted to socialize children. Each activity has socializing agents, teacher or peer, a defined direction for action, and a specific time and place which provides a structure for each activity, allowing each participant to project meaning on to it. The nature of children's responses to classroom activities indicated varying stages of acculturation on the part of the children. Teachers need to know whether or not children learned; that is determined by the children's ability to do what was expected of them. Everything outside of the classroom being equal, in school some Secoya children performed at grade level in a classroom where their friends were underachieving. This showed only that some children had internalized the school's expectations and had learned to compete, while other children had not yet learned what was expected of them, much less how to accomplish it.

The nature of the classroom activities revealed that children learned the lesson according to the degree that they participated in it. Pattern of activities showed what teachers considered important as content and format in the daily instruction. Every activity had definable characteristics including the people involved, time and place, the goals of the lesson, as well as the meaning of the activity.

Practice Drills

The most common type of lesson observed during reading and math was the rote drill exercise where students were expected to produce one-letter, one-word or one-number answers to the teacher's questions. The emphasis in these lessons was on the memorization of words or numbers or phrases out of context. The English as a Second Language activities were typical of the lessons in the classification. During the course of these lessons teachers modeled for students the actual phrases which they wanted them to repeat. Sometimes they showed small pictures from the Idea Kit I to the students and told them to name the picture and use it in a sentence, as in the following example. The second grade teacher at Gardner sat in a circle facing a semi-circle of eight students where she showed several 3 × 5-inch cards with pictures of children in various activities. The lesson was on pronouns. She showed the students a card and she modeled what she wanted the children to say.

> Teacher: (Holding up the card) The boys are skating around the tree.
> Group: (In unison) The boys are skating around the tree.
> Teacher: Adriana, What are the boys doing?
> Adriana: Skating around the tree.
> Teacher: (at Adriana) Say, they're skating around the tree.
> Adriana: They're skating around the tree.
> Teacher: Everyone, again, They're skating around the tree.

The teacher drilled the children with about seven cards of similar action pictures. The children repeated as she modeled.

Throughout the lesson, she shifted between describing the pictures using actual nouns and pronouns without explaining the connection to the children. The children repeated as she modeled but used the pronoun form when they answered her question. The teacher began by modeling, 'The boys are skating around the tree.' She then changed the nouns to pronouns when she asked Adriana to repeat the statement correctly.

While the ESL example was an oral drill, such practices were also written and sometimes both media were employed as the teacher guided the students in filling out a ditto sheet with missing words or numbers. Sometimes children were called to the board to demonstrate how to write a particular word while other children wrote it on their sheets. In this example, the teacher assistant tested the children's knowledge of initial sounds in Jesus's class.

> Teacher assistant: ¿Jesus, cómo comienza la palabra 'manzana'? (How does the word 'apple' begin?)
> (Jesus walks up to the board and writes the letter 'M', then returns to his seat.)
> Teacher assistant: Si, asi, 'M'. ¿Ahora quién sabe cómo comienza la palabra 'mundo'? (Yes, that's right, 'M'. Now who knows how the word 'world' begins.)
> (All the children raise their hands, eager to show.)
> Teacher assistant: Gloria, ven a poner la letra en la pizarra. (Gloria come and write the word on the board.)
> (Gloria goes up to the board and writes the letter 'M' then returns to her seat.)

This particular exercise was fifteen minutes in duration as the teacher assistant worked down a list of words in the children's workbook. After they completed the board demonstration part of the lesson, the children were asked to circle the initial letters of the given words in their workbook. They were to do so individually at their desks. A variation to this activity had the teacher dictating words to the children as they wrote the initial sound, word or number on their paper. Even during the independent part of lesson the teacher monitored the children's work to make sure that they were moving along and completing the assignment before they went out for recess.

Whole Class Instruction

In the absence of a teacher assistant to help with the class, teachers conducted full class instruction for most subjects except reading. During full class instruction, all students were given the same assignment: the same math ditto on fractions, the same handwriting lesson and an equal amount of time to complete it. In the following illustration, the third grade teacher presented a set of multiplication problems to the whole class and called on the class as a whole to answer the questions as she asked them.

Children raised their hands if they wanted to volunteer an answer. 'What's the answer to this problem, [15 × 3]?' The teacher called on a student and told the class that they should multiply three by five first, then the carry the one and multiply the three by one and add the one that was carried. She illustrated the calculations for the problem on the board. Following five of these examples, she gave all the class one sheet of multiplication problems and told them to work quietly at their seats. She then called up a small group of students to work on subtraction up at the front table with her.

The rest of the class was left alone to fill out a ditto. All of the students sat at their desks to complete their assignment. Most of the children began working immediately. One girl, Tina, turned to another across the aisle from her and motioned to her to pass an eraser. The second girl, Maria, handed her the eraser and at that point the teacher looked up and asked, 'What's all the commotion about over there, Tina and Maria?' Maria said that Tina had asked her for an eraser. The teacher said, 'All right, give it to her and let's get on with the work.'

The teacher finished with the small group in the front of the class after twenty minutes. She then began to walk up and down the aisles checking students' papers and answering questions for those who raised their hands. While she leaned over to help a student, one Spanish-speaking boy motioned to another Spanish-speaking boy by holding up his hand to indicate the number eight and the other boy whispered forty-eight. The teacher did not address the two boys directly but she raised her head and reminded the class, 'Let's try and do our own work and not bother others.' Other children passed papers back and forth and tried to get answers from their friends rather than ask the teacher. Although many children did ask the teacher directly as she walked around the class, some did not wait for her to get to them and asked other children instead.

The rules for how the work was to be completed were clear in the way that the teacher instructed the children. The specific rules were: No talking. Stay in your seats. No copying. The teacher-directed lesson makes it impossible to manage the class since the teacher instructs the full class and constantly reminded the class to behave. She noticed almost every move that the children made.

The children tried to comply with the teachers' expectations. Children may know what to do but need to check with others for clarification. How children dealt with confusion in their assignments reflects the way that the classroom activities either allowed or repressed children's access to thinking. In many tasks children were instructed in a large group and then assigned individual seat work, and the teacher worked with small groups before supervising the students at their seats.

In Ramona's third grade class the teacher read in English with a group of students at a table in front of the room while the bilingual teacher assistant read with the Spanish group. Ramona had an assignment in her English workbook. Romona tried to ask the teacher for assistance and was turned away because the teacher did not want to be interrupted. Ramona returned to her seat and leaned toward the boy sitting behind her and asked what they had to do on that page, whether it was to circle a word or write it out. In Spanish the boy said, 'Yo creo que debemos de ponerle las palabras en la otra página.' (I think that we're supposed to write the words like the other page.) Ramona asked how he knew that it was the way it should be. Just then, the teacher saw the students whispering back and forth and called to her with a question. 'What are you doing back there, Ramona? You don't need to be talking, if you can't figure it out, don't bother Jorge.' Ramona returned to her book and continued to fill in the words as Jorge had interpreted the assignment.

She had tried to understand how to do the task according to instructions, but the teacher's message was that it was more important for her to try and do it by herself whether she understood or not. Often the messages conflicted when teachers emphasized that it was important to get it right; the consequences would be to stay in at recess and repeat the work. Students attempted to fulfill the teacher's expectations, but they found it convenient and necessary to share information. The children viewed each other as natural resources to accomplish their task. Ramona coped especially well in trying to get assistance. Her work was usually done correctly. Ramona's and Tomás' request to get an example from their classmates indicated a need to understand as opposed to the teachers' perception that students who wanted to work with each other did it to 'copy' from each other.

Trying to figure out how to get the right answer while attempting to respect the classroom rules, to work individually and quietly, sometimes required more time and effort than the worksheet tasks themselves. Trueba (1983) presented the typology of stress levels which Mexican American children experienced as part of their cultural adjustment in the classroom, while attempting to understand how to behave and win approval without knowing how. Such was the case of Jesus who often talked while the teacher explained the assignment. He was also confused about the content in trying to complete the task.

In his first grade, Jesus and other classmates had been assigned three ditto sheets where they had to complete the Spanish words under the pictures. Words included, a _____ (vión), v_____(entana), f_____(lor), (plane, window, flower). Jesus filled in four of the words on his sheet and then looked around to see what others in his group were doing. He caught one boy's attention and asked him if he knew how to spell the rest of the word for (manzana) 'apple'. The boy shrugged his shoulder as if to say that he did not know. Jesus turned his attention to his paper and tried to fill in another word, (arbol) 'tree' and continued to try to find out how to spell apple in Spanish. Just then the teacher called out in Spanish, 'Tienen que terminar antes que salgan al recreo.' (You need to finish your [work] before you go out to recess.) He walked around as if he was going to throw a piece of paper in the wastebasket and stopped at a table to look over a girl's shoulder. She looked up at him and told him that she was going to tell the teacher that he was copying. He walked away and leaned over another boy's desk and asked him for the spelling of 'manzana'. He said he did not know and showed him his paper and told him, 'Así le puse yo.' (That's the way I wrote it.) Jesus looked at it and walked back to his seat. He wrote down what his friend had on his paper. The spelling was correct except they had used an 's' instead of a 'z'. Jesus had succeeded in getting the information he needed, but he had not counted on the teacher seeing him. She called out to him from the small group where she was teaching, 'Jesus put one check by your name on the board for walking around and talking to people.' Jesus looked stoic as he walked up to the board and put the check by his name. For the rest of the class time he sat at his desk and played with his pencil.

Jesus tried to find ways of conforming to the teacher's expectations even when he did not know the subject matter. He found, however, that if he did not know something, he was constrained from figuring it out, because the rules of the class forbid students to talk to others or to get up from their seats. His barriers to learning affected the outcome. When Jesus was reprimanded by the teacher and he knew that he would have to stay in at recess to do his work, he stopped working on his assignment for the rest of the class period.

Using Language and Experience

Although teacher-directed activities in large and small groups often revolved around right or wrong type responses on the part of the children, two teachers at two different schools, (a first grade teacher at Oakgrove and a third grade teacher at Gardner school) valued the children's experience and used it to motivate them to read and write in what is known as the 'Language Experience Approach' or LEA (Dixon and Nessel, 1983). Their approach differed only in that the first grade teacher had the children use a list of words of their own choosing to compose their stories, while the third grade teacher had the children compose their stories from their own experience without prior word lists. They typically used this approach about once a week as part of the reading and language arts program. Although parts of the lesson were conducted under teacher direction, children were allowed to express themselves without fear of being wrong.

The first grade teacher's approach was to have each child in the class keep a list of the words that s/he wanted to learn to spell. They used the same list to compose their stories. In the third grade, however, the purpose of the LEA was for the children to construct a story of their choice following a brief discussion of what they were thinking about. After the story had been written, the teacher sometimes had children share their written stories with each other in small groups. If they did not complete their story within one class period, they were able to continue it the following day.

Alicia was a student in this class. One story she wrote was about her father's new truck. He was a gardener and had to ride quite a distance out of town to the ranch where he worked. Alicia told the story from her viewpoint: how she was happy that her father did not have to be stranded on the road with the old truck when it broke down. Her story was in English. Although she began reading in Spanish, she quickly learned to read well in both English and Spanish.

My father bought a new pick-up truck. This one is more special than the other one we had because he put a camper on it. Now my brothers and I can ride in it without messing up our clothes. I also like it a lot because my father does not have to worry about it when it breaks down on the freeway. I always used to worry and so did my mother because one day he came home very late without his truck and he had to leave the truck in the garage. The first [time] he took me and my brothers [in the truck] was to church where the priest blessed it because my mother was afraid to ride with until it was blessed. [The story was edited for grammar errors only].

In her story, Alicia illustrates her love and concern for her father as well as her excitement about having a camper in which they could ride comfortably. During the writing session, the teacher sometimes walked around to look at their writing and made comments about their spelling, if it needed checking, and also asked the students questions about their spelling and their story to trigger their memory about an event and thus expand their story. For example, Alicia had completed her story up to the point where her father had left his truck at a garage and the teacher asked her where they had gone on their first ride in their new truck. Alicia responded that they had gone to church because her mother said it was not safe to go anywhere until the priest blessed it. Alicia had the opportunity to write about her cultural practices expressed in ways validated by the teacher.

Teachers were the leading authority figures in these class-rooms. In most cases teachers taught the entire class without the help of a teacher assistant. When they had a teacher assistant, they arranged instruction in a way to give time to students in small groups usually. Individual seatwork was also defined by the teachers' rules and tacit curriculum. Instruction in large and small groups and individual structures revealed specific patterns of interaction between the teachers and students and between students.

With the exception of the language experience approach, classroom interaction was restricted to short right/wrong answers. The teacher asked questions and students answered. When the students were allowed to raise their hands and ask clarification questions, only the teachers were allowed to provide assistance. Restricted interaction was controlled by restricted use of space at any given time. Although the lower grade students in the first grade seemed to have more flexibility in selecting work areas, the amount of mobility was related to the level of noise which teachers would permit. Noise was not accepted by any teacher although one first grade and one third grade teacher did not admonish students as severely for talking while working. The rule for 'no talking' and 'no walking around' were independent from any concern for what assistance children needed to understand their assignments and to learn how to think about their work.

Reflections of School Learning

It was sometimes easier to tell what was learned in school by the way children behaved outside of school. Children made sense of what they learned in school by applying it to familiar settings. Schools went home in a number of ways, through behaviors, linguistic practices, attitudes, and occasionally through homework. Parents sometimes helped their children in doing their homework, but mostly they felt that the children knew more than they since they had not been schooled in this country. Although all of these parents were in an evening adult English as a Second Language class once a week, for the most part, they felt incompetent in helping their children with homework. Some parents attended less frequently than others, because sometimes their jobs required them to work longer hours on days which coincided with the class. They did, however, say that they were in class so that they could help their children to succeed since it was no longer possible to achieve any more for themselves, as much as they would like to.

Parents believed that education would promise their children more from life than they had. They wanted their children to do well in school so that they could have better employment opportunities. Although these goals were noble and optimistic, children had to contend with making meaning of their day-to-day activities. Two distinctive cases indicating how children brought school home involved Jesus and Raul and Alicia.

Jesus and Raul attended different schools. Jesus was a first grader in Gardner School and Raul was a repeat second grader in Oakgrove school. However, they knew each other from their favorite 'hang out' place in front of the community center and occasionally saw each other at a church gathering at St. Josephs'. They had friends in common and both could participate in the older boys' groups. The boys occasionally played with children their age, but more often they were found just standing by the groups of junior high and high school boys who 'hung' around the community center listening to large stereo radios. The boys did not interact directly with the older boys except for Raul's older brothers who 'hung' around in the same vicinity. Jesus did not have older brothers but he had, as had Raul, found acceptance by this group of older high school boys. The young boys modeled their behavior at the favorite common places as well as the amount of time they spent just 'hanging out'. These boys' behaviors disrupted their family routine at times because their families expected them home at a particular time but the boys were generally inaccessible. Although Jesus's school absences were verified by his mother as being due to common colds, most of Raul's absences were not substantiated. Although his parents thought he was going to school when they left for work, Raul often decided not to attend school and instead rode around on his bicycle. Jesus's parents had more difficulty with Jesus's behavior at home because they wanted him to do more around the house than Raul's parents. Essentially, both sets of parents were unhappy about their children's unwillingness to conform to either the home's or the school's rules. Parents wanted the boys to respect their home rules and to transfer those values to their school behavior.

Alicia, on the other hand, respected her parents and teachers. At home she helped out with the household chores and obeyed all her parents' instructions. She conformed to school rules and was almost a model child: she listened to the teacher, never got her name on the board, advanced well academically and was accepted into the Gifted and Talented Program. After school she went straight home except on the days when she went to catechism at the church. She always completed her homework with her father's assistance and never fought her parents to awaken in the morning.

These cases illustrate that Hispano children can live in the same community and have diverse cultural adaptation patterns as a result of their internalized feelings and perceptions about their home and school experiences. In the case of Raul and Jesus, they both had rather negative experiences in the school which made them feel inadequate. Their lack of self-esteem in the classroom was recovered by their 'hanging out' with the older boys and gaining status lost in their humiliation at school. The absence of respect for authority was the most difficult part for the boys' parents to accept. They believed that their children were losing the family's cultural values and that both family and school had failed them. The boys' cases illustrated that the children's behavior out of school was antagonistic to what parents and teachers expected in their respective settings. Their patterns of behavior were beyond the parents and teachers' control. Alicia was the model child who wanted no more than the approval of the adults around her. The point in this comparison is that the children in both cases sought attention in whatever ways encouraged them. Positive behavior was expected and rewarded in Alicia's case and it seemed to perpetuate itself. The contrary was true in Jesus' and Raul's case who caught people's attention by acting against expectations. The more they were punished by the school authorities, the more they sought to be accepted by adolescents with deviant behavior. At this young age they were already being shunned because their behavior differed from the school expectations. Needless to say, we cannot advocate that the school should not admonish children who do not follow rules. The consistent rule in the school where these children were concerned, however, seemed to be that children whose values and behavior were congruent with what the school expected got through with little trouble, while children who had difficulty following the school rules were considered 'problems'. Discipline and academic problems overlapped and they perpetuated one another.

Parental Expectations of Schools

All the parents believed that education was important. The importance of schooling differed for the families only in emphasis. Generally they expected their children to take advantage of every day of their schooling so that they could find a good job. Parents clearly believed that their children had an opportunity which they had missed and that as parents they would do all they could to get their children to school. They viewed education as an activity in which the children received preparation for a career while learning to maintain and respect parents' values. They wanted their children to be respectful to adults not only at home but at school. Parents used their own interactions with their children at home as a measure of comparison for the lack of teachers' emphasis on respect at school. Furthermore, they feared that their young children would become like the Cholos who hung out at the street corners. They felt that they were strict with their children and tried to get their children to share and talk kindly to others. A major discontent with most parents was that they believed that schools were far too permissive with children, especially if children were disrespectful to them at home. Even parents of children who usually received positive reports about their behavior criticized the teachers for not teaching children how to respect their elders.

Speaking Spanish was another way in which parents evaluated the merits of their children's schooling experience. Parents valued bilingualism (Spanish and English) because they believed that their children had to continue communicating with them and other family members in Spanish and they also felt that bilingualism was a desirable skill for employment. So strong was the parents' desire for their children to maintain Spanish, that they pretended not to understand English so their children would speak to them in Spanish. Mrs. Gomez comments:

> Yo a veces me hago que no entiendo inglés para que me hable en español. Mi hijo Jesus, ya comienza a hablarme en inglés y le digo que me cuente todo lo que quiera pero no va recibir nada de mí si no me habla en español.

> (Sometimes I pretend that I don't understand what he's saying so that he will talk to me in Spanish. My son, Jesus, already begins to talk to me in English and tells me anything he wants except that he won't get me to give him anything unless he talks to me in Spanish.)

Parents' commitment to ensure that children retain Spanish was by no means one-sided. Some parents took English classes and let their children know that they were trying to help them in their school work. On occasion children brought home school work that required English skills, and parents wanted to try some way to understand what their children were doing at school. Most parents that enrolled in English classes, however, believed that the chances were minimal for them to learn English well enough to change their own economic conditions. They did, however, want their children to see that they were making an effort to learn, even though they had monumental inconveniences like time constraints and childcare problems. More than anything parents wanted the freedom to move about their daily interactions confidently without a translator in institutions where Spanish was not spoken.

Homework and school performance caught the attention of parents when teachers sent home report cards or when they called the home to complain about a student's classroom behavior. Parents seldom punished their children for not doing their school work or for receiving bad grades in school. Poor behavior in school was, however, reprimanded. When children misbehaved in school, it was considered a serious offense for the parents. They believed that the family was shamed by their bad behavior in school.

Parents rewarded children for receiving good grades at school although they usually did not know at what level their children performed. That is, some students received a 'B' letter grade for reading while they were in a reading group below their grade level, as in the case of Mario. Rewards were also given for tasks like completion of homework and 'A' grades in report cards. If there was any pattern to the homework activities, it was that the more advanced students were usually given more homework than other students. This practice differed significantly with the findings of a study of linguistic minority children in another California community where children in the low reading groups received more homework than those in the high groups (Delgado-Gaitan, 1990). Hugs, kisses, special food treats, special outings and small gifts like booklets, storybooks or shoes constituted rewards for good grades and good behavior at school. Rewards helped to seal a common understanding between the children and their parents that doing well in school was important.

Parents in School

The school district provided a special English as a Second Language night class for parents of limited English-speaking students. The project lasted two years. The cohort involved in this study participated in that year-long class. Parents were recruited from the three elementary schools in the districts that were highly impacted with linguistically different students. The goal of the class was to teach the parents to read in English by beginning with their first language. They were also supposed to learn how to work with their children on homework tasks. Classes were held twice a week for 2½ hours each class.

Activities centered around whole class instruction by the teachers who used small picture cards to model sentences and elicit responses. For example, the lesson was about the plural form. The teacher held up a picture card of a dog and modeled, 'This is a dog.' Immediately following, she held up a card with several dogs and said, 'Dogs, these are dogs.' and the parents repeated. If this scenario resembles that of the children's classes, it is because the materials for this adult class were used to correspond to those used to teach children's English as a Second Language lessons in the elementary schools. Adults also worked in self-paced reading workbooks. When they reached a given level, parents were moved from reading in Spanish to reading in English. Actually the average growth for parents was two years of reading in Spanish and one and a half years in English if they attended regularly. Missing in the project was an emphasis on ways to help children in homework tasks aside from occasional contrived activities designed by the ESL teacher and carried out by the parents and their children during a forty minute period as part of the adult class time.

In spite of the fact that the classes did not enforce a strong component of how adults could work with their children with homework tasks, parents believed that for them learning English was important because of their family. Prior to beginning the English literacy classes, parents varied in their ability to help their children with their homework. For some parents, it was a time of frustration and guilt, when and if their children received homework, because they could not help them; others took the time to assist their children within their ability, while other parents believed that their children could do their work better without intervention. As a result of the class, only some parents increased the time spent with their children at homework, becoming aware of the need to supervise their children's work. The problem that persisted relative to homework was the way in which the homework was assigned that gave preference to children who were more advanced. As a general practice teachers did not assign homework to students who did not return their homework. This perpetuated a belief that some children were capable and others not. Without understanding how homework was distributed according to teachers' perceptions of children's capabilities, parents assumed that their children did not receive homework because they were doing well in school.

Parents who wanted to learn how to better help their children in their homework believed that attending English literacy classes would expand their ability to help their children with their schoolwork. Parents who did not help their children directly also expected to learn English, but they did not have specific intentions to help their children in schoolwork, rather, the parents wanted to learn English so that they could be more autonomous in their interaction with institutions. Many of the older children were the interpreters between their parents and institutions. Many parents felt that their freedom and privacy depended on learning English so that they could conduct their business without depending on their children. Regardless of how parents perceived their gains in the English classes, they all agreed on one point: they wanted to learn English to help their children, because while it was too late for the parents to get better jobs, if their children could learn both languages there was hope for them to obtain better employment.

Summary

Just as knowledge acquired in the family setting in home influences children's school behavior and practices, so do classroom activities impact how children perceive themselves and their world outside of school. The learning cycle between the home and school is so much of a natural process that it is difficult to ascertain the specific factors that effect the cycle. Understanding the process of learning between home and school and back requires an examination of activity organization patterns and the meaning of the practices. Meaning is inherent in the socialization process. Children came from homes where they share in responsibility, leadership, curiosity for learning and exploration. Above all, love and respect for one another governed their activities. From an educational point of view, children were prepared to learn when they arrived in school. Teachers, with few exceptions, ignored what children brought to school and interpreted their differences as deficiencies which had to be repaired through formulaic repetition drills. Although some teachers attempted to depart from this mode of instruction, they faced limitations of insufficient training compounded by professional values that give preference to enforcing rules and making sure students remained on task. The best of intentions on the part of teachers cannot compensate for the way that the teachers' education system fails them. Teachers are not prepared for the challenges of teaching children, who from their perspective seem to be failures, when in fact these children possess a wealth of knowledge and skills which can be harnessed and transformed into creative ideas, as one of the teachers attempted to do through writing exercises. As parents became students in English, they too became acquainted, although in a limited way, with their potential for learning as well as that of their children. The only problem here was the brief exposure to the new ideas of what education is in the US. Their involvement needed to be a systematic and sustained effort. The point is that just as children need to be incorporated into the learning process as active participants, so do their parents because they are the principal parties responsible for socializing children.

Chapter 6

Towards an Ethnography of Empowerment

Chapters Two through Five described the substance of an ethnographic study of Hispano children transitioning from the home learning environment to that of school. The authors want to argue that the ethnographic research conducted here has two important functions. The first function is to help develop conceptual knowledge based on different methodological and theoretical assumptions. These assumptions constitute a research approach that not only recognizes a close relationship with empirical data bases (in the ethnographic jargon, it is 'grounded' research), but it recognizes the impact of data bases in the reorganization of knowledge and the conceptual frameworks or cognitive categories resulting from such reorganization. Specifically, the study focuses on the critical role that the home culture and language have for the understanding of the process of cultural integration Hispano children experience, and the significance of the home learning environment as an essential component of children's learning. The second function is to recognize that this conceptual framework used to analyze the data has implications for practice and provides practitioners with important ideas guiding the implementation of educational reform. Chapter Six discusses the first function, the relevance of this ethnographic research project for theory building, and chapter Seven discusses the practical implications of this research project for educational reform and daily practice. First, however, an ethnography of empowerment requires some discussion of the central concepts of empowerment, disempowerment, and power.

The Process of Empowerment

Empowerment means the process of acquiring power, or the process of transition from lack of control to the acquisition of control over one's life and immediate environment. Therefore, empowerment is equated with the possession of power to act or to effect something by participating in a given activity, or by acquiring social status associated with the enjoyment of human rights and privileges universally and crossculturally recognized as universally accorded to all members of the human race. Empowerment as applied to teachers in their professional career has been discussed recently:

> Professional empowerment is not a privilege of the collectivity of teachers, much less a privilege granted teachers by the power of central government offices. Professional empowerment is understood here to involve the individual teacher's possession of the conditions, means, knowledge, and skills required to teach, it is understood as a right similar to the rights of other professionals (Trueba, 1989:148).

Beyond this concept of fundamental right to the means required for competent professional performance, the concept of empowerment is more encompassing as it links psychological processes (internalization of knowledge through critical thinking) with the social reality in which the individual functions. In this sense, Delgado–Gaitan (1990) discussed the process of empowerment for Mexican American families through the acquisition of English literacy. The ability of parents and their children to acquire new knowledge about the social reality of the United States, and to do this through text, is truly a significant emancipatory event. The reason is that knowledge had been inaccessible to parents previously because of the double barrier of their illiteracy and their lack of the English language.

Viewed from the perspective of an individual becoming engaged in the process of empowerment, be that of an individual teacher, a parent or a child, empowerment is constituted by a series of social, and psychological events that have political consequences because they lead to the important realization that the individual can control his or her own destiny by controlling access to knowledge. This knowledge starts within the self, and the place of the individual in a given society. One's own place in society cannot be surrendered. It must be defended by exercising the right to participate in the social, legal, political and economic systems which determine individual status and his/her access to knowledge or other forms of power.

As Barr has eloquently stated, 'The literature on power is vast, covering hundreds of years of writing and drawing upon five primary disciplinary fields; philosophy, political science, sociology, psychology and economics' (1989:1–2). The questions addressed by these fields discusses the means to obtain power and to hold on to it, the relationship between power and morality, the corruption associated with holding power, the meaning and extent of exercising power, and the sources and instruments of power. In the sixteenth century Machiavelli offered good advice to powerholders; in the seventeenth century, Hobbes discussed the use of power to obtain personal pleasure. Both Machiavelli and Hobbes saw the use of individual power as the political arena for conflict and competition. Nietzsche in the nineteenth and twentieth centuries saw power as related to the self-worth of the individual. According to Barr's interpretation of Nietzsche 'to want power to do evil was a sign of weakness and low self-esteem' (1989:4).

Sociological thinking on power in American society is characterized by two opposite views, the rationalist and the utopian. According to Barr the 'rationalist believes conflict and competition are essential to the nature of power in a social system' and power is intrinsically coercive in nature; consequently 'coercion is an essential aspect of all power relationships' (1989:5). Within this view power necessarily occupies a predominant place in all social systems and functions and becomes an independent social variable. Power can 'take on numerous symbolic meanings, for example, money, land, and knowledge' and the monopoly of power in the hands of an elite 'creates in the powerless a sense of alienation and frustration over their lack of power' because power elites are uncontrollable except in the face of generalized conflict created by the powerless (Barr, 1989:5–6).

In contrast, the utopians do not see power as control over other people, but as the ability to accomplish something, or 'power to do' rather than 'power over others'. Barr sees utopian power as built around trust and furthering communal interests to 'fulfill binding obligations' in a setting characterized by an 'element of accountability that keeps powerholders in check' (Barr, 1989:6). For the rationalists, there is no possible accountability of the powerful to anyone. For the utopians the powerful are accountable to the community and use it primarily to deal with new and changing situations.

The use of power, and consequently empowerment as the process to gain access to power, is not only a sociological or cultural reality, but a psychological one affecting individual self-concept and behavior. As a psychological process, empowerment can affect an individual or a group of individuals in gaining control over their own destiny, specifically by determining their degree of participation in democratic institutions. This participation in democratic institutions is gained (or regained) through study of, and reflection on, the place historically occupied by individuals in the social and economic strata of societal institutions. Consciousness of the nature of inalienable human rights that are inherent to members of the human species regardless of sociocultural, political, economic, religious, racial or social status differences, is clearly at the heart of empowerment.

There is a very close relationship between the processes of empowerment and disempowerment. Both are linked to the social construction of reality in an stratified society with differential access to power. The psychological phenomena accompanying disempowerment processes — for example, in the form of asymmetrical power relationship which include systematic exposure to degradation incidents and prejudicial treatment — affect profoundly the self-concept and personality structure of the individuals being disempowered. Victims of prejudicial treatment (DeVos, 1973, 1983, 1988) experience a gradual internalization of the negative attributes ascribed to them by the powerholders. Thus individuals of low status develop a low self-esteem, a feeling of incompetence, and a sense of helplessness.

The process of empowerment is the mirror image and must follow steps that reverse the previous trends. Disempowered individuals must redefine their experience of prejudicial treatments in ways that do not reflect personal fault or limitations of the victim. These experiences must be counteracted by positive experiences interpreted as success, high status and recognition in social settings. As previous victims regain self-confidence and esteem, they can also begin to act out their new self-confidence in social interactional settings. If we describe the process of disempowerment as a type of socialization which results in lack of self-confidence, in psychological and sociocultural conflicts, and ultimately in failure to participate meaningfully in social institutions, we can also describe empowerment as the opposite socialization process whereby individuals internalize high self-esteem, ability to function effectively, confidence to work well, and the creation of opportunities to find access to information and resources enhancing individual or collective goals. The construction of failure parallels the construction of success in the same social structural settings and cultural units where individuals learn to function and behave appropriately, such as the family, schools, and other public settings (Trueba, 1988a:210–211).

The present study of children's cultural transition from the home learning environment to that of school, indeed to that of the dominant society, can be considered one of the studies constituting the Ethnography of Empowerment. In the last ten years, the literature of empowerment has extended from family studies, intervention models in the health sciences, and psychological research, to studies of learning environments with clear implications for the acquisition of literacy and effective academic learning in schools. Such theoretical directions have been led by work based Freire's *Pedagogy of the Oppressed*, (1970); and on the work by Solomon, (1976), Rappaport, (1981); and others including the Cornell Empowerment Group, (Allen, Barr, Cochran, Dean, and Greene, 1989).

Delgado-Gaitan (1990) has also advanced the specific nature of the relationship between literacy acquisition processes in children with their parents' process of empowerment to function effectively in public institutions other than school. What has not been defined clearly in the anthropological literature is the over-all umbrella of studies conducted via ethnographic methods dealing with empowerment issues in education. Educational anthropology has come of age and as such has impacted the discourse on the nature of mankind and the processes whereby humans learn to behave as humans and transfer knowledge and values from one generation to another. Ethnographic research, as an elusive and increasingly more controversial instrument (used by scholars from a number of disciplines and with diverse theoretical frameworks), is now recognized as a unique instru-ment to study the process of empowerment. This chapter attempts to clarify the concept of empowerment in educational anthropological contexts, and to propose the parameters for an ethnography of empowerment with focus on education.

Lessons Learned in this Study

Children's interactions in their home, community and classroom enhances their ability to learn within the respective conditions in those respective settings. In Neo-Vygotskian theory it is assumed that cognitive development consists of an increased ability to manipulate symbols (particularly linguistic symbols) both for intra-psychological and inter-psychological functions (Wertsch, 1985). Considering the sociocultural environment sur-rounding children and their families, we can account for the variation of material and socioeconomic factors which influence a family's social construction process (Bernheimer, Gallimore and Weisner, 1989). DeVos' work consistently points to the realization that the appropriate interpretation of people's use of linguistic symbols is found first in broader culturally patterned social structures and later in the context-specific behaviors which can be observed by means of ethnographic methods. Vygotsky (1978) viewed language as a symbolic system mediat-ing thought and action, as well as an instrument for the develop-ment of thinking skills. Thus, the mastery of language was seen by Vygotsky as a measure of mental development. He empha-sized the active role of the learner in determining his/her area of most probable cognitive development, which he called the Zone of Proximal Development (ZPD). The learner must exercise control of his ZPD through linguistic responses during learning activities. This behavior is evident in activities that provide the child with a place to belong as a family or community member. The role that culture plays in social activities is seen through the joint construction of communication and knowledge by adults and children. Activities in the children's home, community and classroom provide an insight into just how such learning occurs.

Children's Enduring Self: Patterns in Sociocultural Change

The study describes the rich linguistic and cultural milieu of the children in their homes and community and results in indisputable findings that these children and their families are not deficient linguistically, culturally, or cognitively. The school, however, in spite of a general interest on the part of the children to attend, remains an alien place for many of the children in terms of incorporating children's cultural knowledge, values and language to enable them to learn by building on their own knowledge. Generally speaking, this relegates these children to a position of having to catch up to their Anglo counterparts who have an advantage simply because they speak English, the standard language of schooling. In addition, the classroom curriculum is organized more to correspond to Anglo mainstream values than to reflect a variety of other preferences. Yet some Hispano children in this study were achieving in school in spite of the fact that they spoke only Spanish in the home, and had social networks with other children who did not perform well in school.

Clearly the underlying premise here is not a simplistic synchronic one-to-one correspondence of cultural congruence between the child's ability to speak Spanish in the home and English in school or the use of social networks in the community versus the individualistic values of the classroom. Variation can be explained in a number of ways. Primarily we need to recognize inter-ethnic variation in a historical perspective. Each of the children in this study and their families had a unique experience in the United States. Some children's families had extensive contact with Secoya prior to their official immigration which contributed to their accelerated adjustment to language and sociocultural forces which led to increased cognitive development as a result of more knowledgeable family support systems and learned strategies for coping with culturally different institutions like the school.

Hispano children of immigrant parents have experiences different from Anglo mainstream children for a variety of reasons. While there may appear to be some general characteristics among Spanish-speaking children, in fact little could be generalized about these children as a cohort. The children in this study had little in common other than the fact that they had similar play interests outside of school. Some of the children did well in school, others did not; some children helped in the home, others helped less.

Their proficiency in Spanish and minimal command of English contributed to the difficulty in sociocultural and psychological adjustment. Their adjustment is compounded by institutional neglect, poverty and exploitation suffered by the entire family. Little privacy exists in crowded dwellings. Many lack proper medical care and services. Children may go without shoes, clean clothes and even proper meals if parents work long hours in two or more jobs to make ends meet. Nothing seems to jeopardize their mental development more than the cultural and linguistic isolation they suffer as a result of poverty.

The isolation entails cognitive neglect, limited opportunities at home to acquire learning and critical thinking skills and to internalize those values. As these children compare their life at home with that of their community friends and those at school, they confront feelings of low self-esteem in their inability to keep up with the school work although, for the most part, they liked school. Fortunately, many children from this background broke their isolation by becoming involved as cultural brokers in their homes, and as translators for their parents as Marcos, Marina, Saul and other older children in the family did.

Collectivity and Individual Skill

The term collective presumes an opposite to the term, i.e. individual. Children's interactions in their home and community sharply contrasted with interactions in their classrooms. At home they helped out with the household chores usually as a result of a request by their parents. The approach to the tasks usually involved a sibling or friend. Children's collective orientation to their work met with approval and encouragement from their parents. In some instances parents required children to work together, but often children accepted the parents' assignments and engaged their friends to assist them. Their individual skills were developed in chase games and other physical skill play that highlighted individual children's skills. While individuals demonstrated their skills, the person who was able shared their skills with others in home and play activities. Classroom lessons, however, did not openly allow children who knew more to share their knowledge with others. Children displayed confidence in their activities outside of the classroom. Winning in games meant victory for all. Children confidently competed against themselves more than they did against each other. In the school setting, however, competition meant that only the 'best' won. There was no room for more than the 'best' whether it was the individual or group. Thus, children's sense of self-worth was dependent on the teachers' ability to construct activities that did not undermine their collective skills in sharing.

Leadership and Turn-Taking

Children used their homes, streets, buildings and other areas of their community as playgrounds in which to organize their play activities. Leadership was assumed by all children in different games depending on the children's abilities, interests and opportunities to engage others in play. Children of all ages and genders had the opportunity to lead others in activities which they knew best. While some children were not strong runners, they had opportunity to demonstrate their knowledge about how the social system functioned. They dealt with banks, hospitals, stores, recreation facilities, churches, businesses and other social institutions. They learned that in order to become competent communicators, they must acquire English literacy. These children, however, did not have the adult models at home to teach them, only to expect them to interpret. In fact, children functioned as adults in translating for their parents and advising them regarding appropriate responses to representatives of public institutions. Before children reached school age, they had internalized racism through their parents' activities. The rejection and/or suspicion which parents faced were felt by the children. The unfair treatment which parents confronted in the work place or in other institutions influenced children's views of American society around them and contributed to their perception of hostility in their early school encounters. To the benefit of the younger siblings, this initial adjustment phase does not affect equally all children in the family.

Some older siblings undertook responsibilities at home that many younger siblings rarely did. Such dealings with the various institutions made it necessary to retain bilingual and bicultural skills in order to be effective translators and advisors at their young age. Unfortunately, the school failed to capitalize on these children's leadership skills. In classrooms, children were all relegated to subordinate positions where they were not expected to think for themselves. Not only did they have to wait for the teachers' instructions to do a task, but the tasks themselves never required them to use more than a low-level recall skill.

Using and Learning Language

Children's language and opportunities for development of higher cognitive skills were much richer in their home and communities than in the classroom. Their collective work with siblings and/or friends at home created contexts for children to share in the division of labor and to jointly negotiate the level of work. Their dramatic storytelling as well as other verbal games in the community illustrated verbal and cultural knowledge as well as leadership ability as they staged their lore with their friends. Conversely, classroom talk was restricted to minimal production while they listened to the teachers who had the only unlimited authority to 'get the floor' (Philips, 1983). Another area where conscious and unconscious uses of language and culture as bases for power struggle is seen is in the range of the ability of the teachers to deal effectively with children whose educational needs challenged their limited training and repertoire of culture in the classroom.

An important point to note is the relationship between the home and classroom values and practices. For example, past theories have insisted that because ethnically different families interact in more authoritarian style, that the teacher's style should correspond with the authoritarian organization of the home. This approach has many problems both theoretically as well as pedagogically. The strict cultural congruence-incongruence model makes the statement that children are the deficient and cannot learn unless taught in the familiar way of the home. Furthermore, teachers can become confused about the specific cultural practice of each child's home especially in classrooms where the ethnic composition varies as much as the achievement levels. We cannot get stuck in one-to-one match between family and community practices with those of the classroom because of the complexity of culture and learning. If we reduce home culture to static stereotypic attributes and expect teachers to organize classroom into static arrangements, the continuous reflection necessary in the teaching process is lost. That is, if we generalize these children's ways of learning outside of the class-room to merely a simplistic notion of cooperative behavior because they play and work collectively, we run the danger of stereotyping the children as monolithic in their learning reper-toire.

For children strategies used to manage their social compe-tence in activities have implicit status and power within each strategies are perceived to have less value than other strategies strategies and perceived to have less value than other strategies as occurs in the school. This contention for power is probably not conscious for most of these children and their families on a day-to-day basis but noticeable nonetheless. Seemingly, every day children face classroom situations where they must choose whether to extend help to a classmate and face getting into trouble for talking with others and not doing their own work, and in some cases, being accused of copying and thereby reprimanded. In those instances, children were not necessarily consciously rebelling against the system, rather they acted naturally as their home and play patterns dictated. Yet, the way that children acted covertly to assist each other indicated their knowledge of classroom rules and willingness to conform to them while trying to help their friends. The issue, then becomes the quality of the classroom interaction allowed both formally and informally by teachers. More conscious levels of power conflicts occurred with children like Raul who openly defied family expectations and school rules as evidenced by his chronic absenteeism at school.

Many children are capable of performing while they may not be learning. In essence they are 'passing' (Rueda and Mehan, 1988), that is, they have learned how to follow rules enough to 'get by'. They have not, however, learned how to operate independently. The lack of culturally appropriate mechanisms to ease the transition from home to school created conflict for some of the children. Rejection of their language and culture may have been inevitable for some of the children, but others did not forget their culture at home. They continued speaking Spanish, practicing oral folklore and respecting their parents' authority. Yet, what was taught in school had little value and application for them in their home and community because it was taught without placement in meaningful context.

By using Spanish outside of school, children reasserted their own identity and expressed subtle rejection of English. Trueba (1983) concluded that in the classroom, Mexican-American children who face cultural conflict may reason in a hyper-participative and hostile way as did Mario, who found his work very frustrating and fought with many of his friends. When children could no longer fight the teacher and the class rules, they assumed a position of isolation or hypo-participation as in the case of Jesus and Raul. Children's achievement motivation would have been more clearly understood had projective techniques been used in this study to explore the issue from the perspective of parents' adaptation patterns and their own cultural values in the US.

Towards an Ethnography of Empowerment

The purpose of this section is to examine the concept of empowerment in educational research contexts, and to propose the parameters for an ethnography of empowerment.

The Context of an Ethnography of Empowerment(EoE)

Social, economic and cultural differences from country to country are perceived as crucial factors in immigration movements. The second half of the twentieth century has seen an increase in the number of immigrant families uprooting themselves from their home country in search of better opportunities. People ,from all over the world immigrate to the United States in search of political, economic and religious freedom for themselves and their children. The Southwestern United States, much of which was originally Mexican territory, has also been quietly 'reconquered' by Spanish-speaking people. Mexicans continue to arrive in ever increasing numbers in California, Arizona, New Mexico, and Texas. They love their country of origin, yet they feel they must seek a solution to their political and economic problems in order to offer their children a better life. Therefore, they come to this country through the Southwest with the commitment to succeed.

The Southwest is also the favorite place for Indochinese and Central American refugee populations who come to this country with terrifying experiences. Freedom and democracy is a matter of life and death, not just a lifestyle which is taken for granted by many American-born citizens. For the newcomers, freedom and democracy translate into due process, respect for individual and family rights, religious freedom, adequate compensation for labor, and respect for human dignity and peace. And all of the above are new experiences that change the lives of refugees drastically and therefore become truly appreciated. In return for the privilege of democracy, immigrants and refugees offer their loyalties and even their lives to America. Their level of motivation to make significant contributions to American social, economic and cultural life surpasses that of many American-born citizens. Perhaps one of the most important contributions made by newcomers to our country is their genuine belief in democratic ideals and active dedication to our democratic institutions.

The study of immigrant and refugee populations is established in anthropology. The emphasis on the cultural adaptation of these populations has been a subject of crosscultural research since the organization of the Human Relations Area Files. The HRAF was the most complete effort in compiling an ethnographic file on all peoples of the world. This effort was spearheaded by George Peter Murdock and his associates in the early 1960s at Yale University. With the help of crosscultural research facilitated through HRAF, anthropologists and other social scientists have studied the process of disempowerment. More recently, educational anthropologists began to pay attention to the response of ethnically and linguistically different students in schools and communities reflecting oppressive social policies, documenting strategies used by minorities to cope with the ensuing cultural conflict resulting from those policies. These efforts constitute 'The Ethnography of Empowerment,' or EoE. The ethnographic work by educational anthropologists developing EoE is eclectic and thus linked to cultural anthropology, social psychology, sociolinguistics and the pedagogical research based both on Paulo Freire's philosophy (Freire, 1970; Freire and Macedo, 1987) and on Spindler's notion of 'Cultural Awareness' or 'Cultural Therapy' (Spindler 1982, 1987).

Ethnographers of empowerment begin with the fundamental assumption that the acquisition of knowledge, or learning, is uniquely human and occurring across cultures primarily in the home or sociocultural units in which individuals are socialized. A second assumption is that learning is purposive and ultimately directed to the enhancement of the cultural values embedded in the content being learned. A third assumption is that learning is mediated by social and cultural frames linked to central concept domains serving functionally as lenses through which new concepts are structured and organized into cohesive units.

Therefore, if we assume that the main motivation of immigrant and refugee families in leaving their home country, their cultural environment and moving to other societies is to seek a better life, that is, freedom or new economic opportunities, then the efforts on the part of these families to uproot their children and leave behind a language, culture, friends, lifestyle and country of origin must be seen as belonging to a superordinate level and perceived by them as of high value. Indeed, their motivation to emigrate is better understood as taking action to satisfy their need to control their destiny, to become empowered in order to deal with scarcity of resources, and with physical or psychological abuse. An ethnography of empowerment, therefore, is based on Freire's notions of social and cultural self-awareness that must aim at developing an ethnohistorical and cultural context to understand the nature of oppression suffered by disempowered people, and the need to create living conditions congruent with the rights of all members of the human species, regardless of ethnicity, color, social status, religion, wealth, political power, knowledge and other personal attributes. The affirmation that an ethnography of empowerment attempts to provide a broad sociocultural context to study the transition from disempowerment to empowerment is very significant, especially if seen as a major effort to create an international database to document population movements across countries and the specific processes of cultural adjustment adopted by these populations.

The significance of EoE goes beyond its pragmatic value in terms of information enriching our minds and explaining waves of change and adaptation in human populations. It redefines the fundamental priorities of anthropological, educational and other social science research by accumulating knowledge with the purpose of improving the living conditions of those being researched. Pursuing knowledge for its own sake is indeed important. However, the pursuit of knowledge for the sake of enhancing human dignity in all humans cannot be subordinated to the obtaining of knowledge for the sake of knowledge. Furthermore, in the study of human behavior, the acquisition of knowledge must be guided by ethical principles and universal cultural values enhancing the survival of the entire human species, and not used to increase the power of some over others, or to perpetuate the oppression of some by others. That kind of research can lead to the ultimate destruction of the human species. Educational research must be reexamined in light of the ethical norms dictating priorities and interests of the entire human species and its solidarity. EoE is a small step towards redefining the collective responsibilities of researchers to their fellow humans. If we recognize the need for an interdisciplinary research on global ecological habitability, then we also need to recognize the importance of interdisciplinary research on social and cultural habitability. Social and cultural structures are often created to perpetuate economic oppression and superiority of one cultural group over others. The resulting asymmetrical power relationships of human groups in their attempts to respond to oppression, and the role of schooling in coping with oppression are critical in contemporary human societies where communications and transnational economic institutions play a key role in maintaining the status quo of those power relationships.

An example of how EoE weaves complex issues in the sociocultural context is found in Delgado-Gaitan's (1990) work. The author uses ethnographic data to explain the role of Mexican parents in their children's acquisition of Spanish and English literacy, and the implications of recognizing the important role parents have in children's cognitive development. By the same token, this volume walks the reader through the day-to-day journey that immigrant children must walk from the home culture to the culture of the school, and the integration of both cultures as they come back home. The critical analysis of literacy events in the context of cultural adaptation and change, of integration of cultural values and the acquisition of new values associated with high levels of literacy — congruent with technologically sophisticated industrial countries as the United States — must be placed in an appropriate theoretical framework. This framework can be labeled 'the Ethnography of Empowerment', or EoE. What are the nature, properties and characteristics of

EoE? The next section is intended to clarify the essential elements of EoE.

Defining the Ethnography of Empowerment

In the anthropological tradition of the last 125 years, ethnographic research must be intrinsically encompassing, holistic, global and systemic. Its first attribute is to provide the reader with an adequate contextualization of the cultural phenomena under study. Likewise, Educational Anthropology has developed over the last thirty years ethnographic research concepts and tools in order to study schooling and learning processes from a broad cultural perspective. Traditionally, ethnographic accounts of schooling and learning in various environments were seen as satisfactory if they portrayed 'objectivity', impersonality, and distance from the populations under study. The outsider's view contrasted with the insider's view, that of the natives in class. The controversy over which one of these views was the most useful, and therefore whether or not doing research in your own backyard was wise, has continued until today. Perhaps, the elusiveness of the 'insider's' and of the 'outsider's' view is here at stake. Empowerment research, especially ethnographic research on schools, must regard the knowledge of children's home language and culture as essential to understanding children's transition from home to school, and the processes of disempowerment (or empowerment) taking place in schools. The misconception that knowledge about the home language and culture of minority children can bias the researcher is as valid as the opposite, that the researcher's own home language and culture can bias her/his research of individuals with a different cultural and linguistic background. Empowerment ethnographic research takes the position that the more you know about the language and culture of immigrant and refugee groups, the better you understand their processes of adaptation and change and the specific phases of adjustment exhibited. Biases come primarily from ignorance.

An ethnography of empowerment, in the tradition of what

could be called the Anthropology of Liberation developed by the Spindlers' 'Cultural Therapy', and of the Consciousness Raising developed by Freire, echoes the efforts of the philosophy postulating the need to integrate cultural values with scientific research. EoE as it has begun to flourish in the last few years can be seen as the emerging methodological and theoretical instrument to build the knowledge base supporting universal human values and the priority of the survival of the human species regardless of color, ethnic, wealth and status differences between subgroups. The peaceful cohabitation of the globe is intimately related to the goals of EoE and of an entire Anthropology of Liberation. Indeed, the body of knowledge comparing and contrasting across nations and sociopolitical systems, the struggles of different cultural and linguistic groups is growing rapidly. These groups strive to reach physical and cultural survival and take steps in search of a nurturing cultural environment in which their human rights are respected and they can enjoy freedom and opportunities to learn and improve their human condition.

In the context of current research conducted by educational anthropologists, EoE can make important contributions to both our understanding of the empowerment process and to the actual achievement of empowerment. EoE is surfacing as the kind of research that focuses on the relationships between social and cultural environments and the acquisition of knowledge for successful adjustment and participation in the benefits of technologically sophisticated societies. EoE can indeed assist educators in handling the problems of 'minority education' and 'cultural diversity' in schools, because it can accomplish the following:

1 Provide a better understanding of the differences between the home and school linguistic and cultural environments in the context of the larger society.
2 Offer a better understanding of the school as a social and cultural reality perceived differently by school personnel and immigrant, refugee and minority communities.
3 Provide appropriate theoretical and methodological approaches to the study of ethnolinguistic, racial and

low-income minority children in schools, with emphasis on their differential academic achievement.

4   Stress the undesirability of the dichotomy between basic (or 'pure') research and applied (or 'mission-oriented') research in the social sciences.

5   Explain the symbiotic relationship between field-based research and theory building.

6   Establish a clear linkage between the macro-structural contexts of behavior (broad historical, political, social or economic data bases), and the actual inferences made by researchers in grounded settings (that is, on the basis of face-to-face observations, interviews and other data gathered).

7   Help design intervention approaches intended to assist refugee, immigrant, racial, ethnolinguistic, and other minority populations to learn to function effectively in schools, hospitals, banks, and other public institutions.

8   Help create data bases from a cross-cultural and trans-national perspective to study the differential adaptation of minority communities in industrial societies.

One of the central thrusts of EoE is on the process of socialization nature, context, agents, circumstances, of minority youth. EoE is a research instrument that can be used to explore changes and transitions of minority youth as they adjust to new and specific cultural contexts with focus on the role of culture or cultural factors in determining, or at least influencing, the processes of socialization. This instrument can help answer such questions as the following: What cultural factors determine the behavioral adaptation and actual performance of Koreans in the United States in contrast with Koreans in Japan?

We assume that a central thrust of EoE is on the role of culture both mainstream and home cultures in determining the nature and extent of participation of minority families in public institutions, as well as on the avenues or mechanisms open for newcomers to cope with cultural conflict. If minorities are pressed hard to adopt mainstream language and cultural values, but they are not accepted as bona fide members of mainstream society, there is a serious conflict in the embedded dilemma of being penalized either way, whether they commit to acculturate or to resist acculturation. Similar dilemmas are faced by newcomers when the cultural values prevalent in the dominant society go through cycles from one extreme to another in the spectrum of tolerance of cultural diversity. At the highest point of intolerance for cultural diversity, newcomers may be perceived as a threat or a handicap rather than an asset, especially during times of political or economic crises. American democratic values are always in a delicate state of equilibrium, continuously being adjusted as the social pendulum moves from tolerance to intolerance triggered by national economic, political and social events.

Empowerment in American Democracy

The study of American culture and society is most complex and difficult. Recently Spindler and Spindler (1990) have discussed the nature of American cultural values and their transmission. They view American democracy as being continuously recreated by the arrival of immigrants with democratic ambitions and the commitment to succeed in America.

Often a group of individuals who have been denied their human rights, for example, the right to move around freely in their own space or in public places, to speak their language, to associate with members of their own ethnic group, to worship, to express their ideas and needs, or to complain about living conditions in which they are forced to live, begin to internalize the oppression of which they are victims as caused by their own deliberate actions and therefore 'deserved.' Or they lose self-confidence and accept their disempowerment as a permanent condition against which nothing can be done. There is, in brief, the possibility that violent or systematic abuse, for example, in the form of consistent degradation, may result in disempowerment of social groups. The social and political realities of exploitation have a high psychological price in the form of devalued self-concept leading to the rejection of one's own language, culture and self-identity.

The denial of human and civil rights and the exploitation of an individual or groups of individuals do not necessarily always result in their psychological disempowerment or the internalization of abuse as a permanent state of affairs. Some individuals (or groups of individuals) manage to retain a high self-concept and a high level of personality integration in situations of oppression or abuse. It is unlikely, but possible, that an oppressive state of affairs in the form of physical coercion and abuse is counterattacked by victims with an increased awareness of one's power and internal freedom. This is possible in a context of social interaction with others through a processs which makes people knowledgeable about the circumstances in which they find themselves and allows for choices about the goals they want to achieve. While choices do not promise achievement of the goals, the liberation process of removing the belief of impossiblity is the central feature of empowerment. Normally, however, systematic, extended denial of human rights tends to be internalized by the victims in the form of personal attributes or deficiencies leading to disempowerment as a permanent reality.

The disempowerment resulting from denial of human rights and abuse of one human being by another is directly related to a social and cultural structural condition of asymmetrical power relationships between individuals or groups of individuals. This means that some individuals are structurally placed to retain the use and abuse of power over others, thus creating a social and cultural arrangement leading to differential access to resources and differential participation in the social benefits of society. Typically, one of the first signs of differential participation is in the access to schools and information bases.

What is still more intriguing is the fact that often the victims of abuse who experience disempowerment are the last to believe that they can get out of that situation and become empowered; that they can learn, acquire the necessary knowledge to participate meaningfully in the social and political process. Systematic degradation tends to disable individuals, thus making it difficult for them to recognize the fact that they are being victimized, or if they do recognize this fact, making it impossible for them to take action in order to prevent further victimization.

The process of disempowerment can take many forms, but

157

often consists of repeated interactions intended to maximize the social and psychological control by the few (the ruling group) over the bodies and minds of other individuals viewed as less valuable and therefore expendable. Members of a ruling group see their subordinates as resource objects whose reason for existence is to serve the purposes of their superiors. Colonial systems and other systems use one form of slavery or another in order to retain structures to perpetuate political and economic advantages, often with support from the government. American democratic institutions and governmental agencies are diametrically opposed to any form of systematic exploitation because a democratic philosophy respects human equality under the constitution. Yet, American history has recorded numerous incidents of civil and human rights violations against citizens who are disempowered. Such protests against injustice protect a democratic form of government clearly advocating equality of rights for all. For example, segregation in housing, public service, schools, and attempts to curtail participation in the political process (attacks on voting rights), or in other social, economic or educational institutions because of creed, race, gender, national origin, or age, is considered unconstitutional because it goes directly against the central cultural value in American democracy, namely that of equal rights for all under the law.

Women's right to vote was not obtained until the late 1920s and only after a general national campaign did the country actually recognize the right. Discrimination against Blacks in schools, restaurants, public transportation and sport was a de facto socially acceptable practice throughout the country until recently (although recognized as unconstitutional in theory). Although human and civil rights are clearly defined there is no guarantee that they will be enforced. National, state and local policies protecting the rights of women and ethnic/linguistic groups often acts only as a window-dressing because they hold little power without the constant monitoring of those affected by them. The importance of EoE is evident when dealing with issues of incongruence between the intent of the policy and its direct impact.

In this study, for the most part, the children were the first generation in the US being raised by the immigrant parents.

Cultural change for this cohort is gradual as opposed to abrupt because the community supports their language, traditions, and style of life. Isolation existed, however, between families and the school as evidenced by the absence of children's culture in the school and respect for differences in learning. Some children do well according the school's evaluation of their achievement which is usually based on the students' ability to comply with the classroom rules. Children can get by, but it does not necessarily mean that learning has occurred. Other children feel isolated already and are aware that they do not fit in at school as early as the second and third grade. What sustains children on a day-to-day basis is a solid sense of self through their ethnic identity, transmitted through values about language, collectivity, respect and emotional support upheld by families and social networks outside of the family including children's play groups. Children learn curiosity, motivation, leadership, cooperation, respect, joy and love through their identity with a family and community. Children's sense of self is a source of power for them as they deal with the classroom routine. It is apparent that neither these children nor their families are deficient in any way except for opportunities to participate in the mainstream culture system.

This brings us to a point that power is context-specific. That is, we cannot discuss power as a monolithic attribute belonging to only one person or group or present in only certain settings. Rather, the force is operative depending on the context and it is utilized differently by players as they attempt to meet their goals in any given activity. Children's activities in their play, for example, illustrate how children use an egalitarian system of interaction with peers as to who defines the play event and how they use turn-taking to engage peers. In their home children negotiate their power with their parents so that parents usually know that their position as parents represents authority over children in decisions about their welfare. That is, children and teachers may interact in a context in which the teacher clearly has the advantage because s/he has organized the setting and can control it. This same teacher may find herself/himself in a teachers' meeting with the principal having to accept the principal's dictates about the textbooks to use in the classroom.

Thus, while children may feel a sense of control in their home and community because they are more familiar with the practices, they may find themselves out of the power group in the school. What they did when they were in control depended on whether they perceive the setting as friendly or hostile. For example, being in a powerful position in activities outside of school had an entirely different connotation than in the classroom. Power was shared in home and community activities while in the classroom, power was a win/lose struggle.

Culture became a source of conflict in the classroom when children's cultural values and language were ignored as they attempted to participate in their own learning. It become apparent that the school failed as an institution capable of providing the diverse settings in which all children could learn without the stigma of being different, because educators tended to view culture in terms of a right-wrong proposition. If the teacher accepted the child's culture, that might mean that the school's middle-class mainstream position was subordinated and devalued. In order to prevent this from happening, the teachers probably believed that they were doing the children a favor by inculcating them into the culture of the school while ignoring their home culture. If we say that empowerment is a process through which people participate in their own learning, then we can be sure that the school is not a place that empowers most of these children. Children are not being empowered in school. A curriculum is imposed on them, which rejects not only their language, but also their need for cognitive development through stimulating engagement in the learning process. In order to have a situation that empowers children in schools, teachers must teach from a strong belief in themselves as individuals and as professionals in high-status positions. As enforcers of the school's philosophy their training, for the most part, has not equipped them with the skills for teaching children of diverse backgrounds. They enter teaching through a societal system that does not value diversity. Additionally, their personal experience includes being students of teachers who had as their goals the instruction of white middle-class students and who had little understanding of or interest in learning how to deal with differences. This brings us to the crucial question: how might the teachers (and ultimately the school) as well as the families become empowered so they can create a viable learning place for this and future generations of children?

Chapter 7

Empowerment and Educational Reform

Poets are exceptional, of course; they are not considered educators in the ordinary sense. But they remind us of absence, ambiguity, embodiments of existential possibility. More often than not they do so with passion; and passion has been called the power of possibility (Greene, 1986:427).

The need for a major theoretical and methodological approach to pedagogical reform in schools and communities has been recognized by researchers. The numbers of reports about the urgent need to resolve our educational problems often ends with sterile allusion to the empowerment of teachers and the need to reform teacher education. Critical pedagogy, either in its radical or in its self-limited version (Gottlieb and La Belle, 1990) is not enough to launch an educational reform intended to change the status of minority group inequity and underachievement solely as a top down effort at the exclusion of the communities involved. As Greene eloquently states:

Of course we want to empower the young for meaningful work, we want to nurture the achievement of diverse literacies. But the world we inhabit is palpably deficient: there are unwarranted inequities, shattered communities and unfulfilled lives. We cannot help but hunger for traces of utopian visions, of critical or dialectical engagements with social and economic realities. And yet, when we reach out, we experience a kind of blankness. We sense people living under a weight, a nameless inertial mass. How are we to justify our concern for their awakening? (Greene, 1986:427).

The role of researchers in educational reform must go beyond traditional evaluation and recommendation patterns based on research models that claim detachment and objectivity through standardized norms to judge performance and a complete detachment from the social and cultural environment in which the educational activities take place. Indeed, a genuine concern for the social and cultural context of learning is intimately related to the profound understanding of the role that culture has in academic achievement. The authors claim that an ethnography of empowerment is one of the most effective instruments for educational reform precisely because it demands critical reflection between the researcher and participants and recognizes the strengths of the families and communities examined to participate in their change. In such cases, educational research is not seen as an instrument to meet the needs of the researcher, but a means to build mutual knowledge for the purpose of engaging communities in their empowerment. This does not mean that researchers govern the change process nor should researchers assume to have the answers to intervene in change of any community's social conditions without the full participation of those affected.

This chapter presents some specific implications of the ethnography of empowerment for efforts to change educational settings in order to make them more responsive to the needs of culturally different children. The value of ethnographic research conducted from an empowerment standpoint is that it elicits data on the nature of cultural conflict faced by students and teachers, and how on the current curriculum is organized to transmit subject matter knowledge to students with other cultural backgrounds and values. More importantly, ethnographic research can play a key role in empowering teachers because it helps them become critical thinkers, conscious of their cultural assumptions and values, sensitive to the values of students whose cultural heritage is in other than middle class mainstream Anglo: It makes them aware of the nature of teaching and learning as a single process in the construction of knowledge. However, the crucial questions regarding the role of ethnographic research on educational reform are the following:

1 What kind of information does ethnographic research pursue that serves empowerment purposes?
2 What is unique about ethnographic research methods that leads to knowledge not obtained any other way?
3 How do we go from ethnographic to reform strategies?
4 How does the implementation of reform measures (as based on the ethnographic study) feed back into theory?

Ethnographic research methods are more time consuming and field labor intensive than other research approaches because researchers need to be in the field for much longer than most other research requires. The study of historical records provides the ethnographer with a context for understanding the setting, the people, and the information provided by the current environment. Participant observation forces the researcher to become involved in activities of the setting under study. From the historical record and initial participant observation encounters, the researchers elaborate a path for getting the information deemed important to gain an understanding of the nature of the community and of the school, in contrast to other schools and communities. Ethnographic interviews allow the researcher to go beyond the information offered by the informants and to probe deeper roots for decision-making, and the overall psychodynamics of reform. Journals and field notes are constant companions that permit the researcher to reflect on what has happened and to search for behavioral patterns. Audio- and video-taping provides the researcher with a record of the events under analysis, in order to examine these events and to study the communication patterns, the linguistic exchanges and the nature of the inferences being made by those who interact. Finally, the ethnographer looks at the entire data for patterns of change and innovation, of conflict and adjustment, of success and of failure in achievement. With the above information, the ethnographer can offer important suggestions for the conceptualization of an intervention intended to improve the quality of instruction in a given school.

What follows are some general remarks about the nature of ethnographic research as applied to empowerment issues. The authors then list some specific ways to use ethnographic studies to conduct change in educational policy and practice.

Ethnographic Research Applied to Reform

Ethnographic research projects are by design long-term and holistic. They attempt to provide a global picture of the historical, social, economic, cultural, and demographic characteristics of schools and communities. As the broader context of the learning environments is built, the linkages between structural (socio-political) factors and specific learning activities in a given setting are established. The analysis of specific teaching/learning events and their consequences are normally contextualized in their broader parameters in order to make sense of long-term trends of performance or achievement. Reform in education has many faces: curriculum, management, fiscal, physical, attitudinal, etc., etc. The rationale for a reform movement in a school or school district must necessarily include trends, processes, distribution of resources, performance, and activities over a period of time and in comparison to other similar units like schools and classrooms.

What ethnographic research can do best is precisely to offer a broader context for the collection and analysis of specific data, and raise a set of questions on assumptions usually neglected in other research designs, for example, questions related to the role of cultural values of both students and school personnel in the performance of both teachers and students. Furthermore, ethnographic research does not just reach a desired outcome and then stop. As ethnographers attempt to answer one question they also formulate subsequent questions in recognition of the information obtained thus far. There is continuous feedback of the knowledge gained into the ongoing research design. The ultimate result of this strategy is that the chains of understanding, the assumptions of a given research project, are calibrated and adjusted as data are obtained.

There is another important characteristic of the ethnography for empowerment. The knowledge generated by ethnographic methods is consistently compared and contrasted in a cross-cultural arena with findings of similar settings and events studied elsewhere. For example, the study of ethnic conflict in Belgium is compared with that of Japan and the United States. Immigration waves and processes of adjustment are compared across countries in an effort to identify structural similarities (power asymmetries) or behavior patterns suggesting comparable processes and responses. The work discussed earlier by DeVos (1980, 1988) and Suárez-Orozco (1987) regarding systematic degradation of ethnic/linguistically different groups suggests similar consequences of self-rejection, disempowerment and cultural conflicts in minorities across cultures. The fundamental problem faced by minorities is making decisions regarding means to empowerment that are not destructive of their ethnic identity and their ties with their community.

A particularly important feature of ethnographic research in the context of empowerment for action is that it creates a climate of critical thinking and self-assessment that prepares the researcher (and teachers as co-researchers in some instances) to recognize cultural differences and biases preventing researchers and teachers from understanding clearly the problems associated with unwillingness or inability to change, or lack of adjustment on the part of parents, children and teachers or other school personnel.

There are many persuasive reasons to embark on school reform. The large increase in ethnically different populations in the nation's largest cities is marked by contrasting trends of neglect and underachievement that threaten the future ability of this country to retain a high technological profile and a strong economy. The case of California, where the present ethnographic study was conducted, is unique because it depicts the future of the entire country. Recent demographic data (California State Department of Education, 1987) shows that for the first time in California's history the White student population is smaller than the ethnically diverse population.

The consequences of underrepresentation of minorities in administrative ranks are devastating for providing adequate attention to the needs of ethnically different students, especially in the organization of curriculum and in the building of community/school cooperative working relationships. Furthermore, neglect of ethnically different students in the early stages of education reduces significantly the numbers in the system for future representation in professional careers and administrative ranks.

Reports generated by national and state organizations and agencies, as well as by various universities, speak to the special need to improve the education of minorities and the overall quality of public schools. By implication it is vital to restructure schools of education in such a way that they become involved in improving the quality of public schools. The quality of education for minorities has increased slightly since 1975 (American Council on Education, 1986; Brown, 1987; Center for Education Statistics 1986; National Research Council, 1986). The academic achievement of precollegiate students and the number of minority PhDs have shown some progress, but the progress is uneven across groups. Asian Americans, and to a much lesser extent Hispanics, account for this increase. Black PhDs have declined in absolute numbers and in proportion to the Black population:

> Compared to earlier cohorts, new ethnic group PhDs in 1986 were older, were less likely to be married, had parents with higher levels of education, and except for Black PhDs, were more frequently male than female . . . Black and Hispanic PhD's were more likely to earn degrees in education and the social sciences, while Asian American PhDs primarily earned their degrees in engineering and the physical and life sciences (Brown, 1988:vi).

Longitudinal tracking of ethnically different faculty in academia revealed that Black PhDs had the lowest promotion and tenure rates among ethnically different groups, and, except for promotions to associate professor rank, their rates were consistently below the national average. Asian Americans had the highest promotion and tenure rates, and both Asian American and Hispanic faculty had promotion and tenure rates above the national average (Brown, 1988:vi).

The persistent underrepresentation of minorities in academia is in clear contrast with the rapid increase of ethnically different school populations and the increasing ethnic diversification of communities in the United States. Consequently, elementary and secondary school children of ethnically diverse groups find themselves without the support, role modeling and curricular adaptations that ethnically different faculty bring to schools. Furthermore, there is an increased isolation of ethnic students who pursue graduate careers and who find the university climate intellectually sterile, racially prejudiced, and altogether unattractive.

These contrasting events — the net decrease of ethnic faculty, in proportion to the existing ethnically diverse population, while the rapid increase of overall ethnic group populations continues — are taking place precisely when the White or mainstream population at large is decreasing. It is expected that before the year 2005 about 40 per cent of the University of California ladder faculty will retire, and that there will be some 10,000 new faculty positions open (Minnis, 1989; University of California Office of the President, 1989a, 1989b, 1989c). The proposed doctoral program emphasizes the preparation of leaders who can bring instructional and institutional effectiveness to public schools. Furthermore, it intends to bring this effectiveness to public schools whose student population is now changing drastically from a mainstream population to one that is highly diversified ethnically, linguistically, socially, culturally and economically. The focus on the characteristics of the new learners in public schools and on instructional effectiveness in basic subjects requires a redirection of research and theory which can best be achieved with a new degree. Indeed, the direction of the proposed doctoral program can establish a national model for needed reorganization of education degrees in the country.

This model should include research and instructional activities in partnerships with the public schools. These partnerships will require a group of specialists who would have a theoretical knowledge of teaching, learning and curriculum as well as practical experience in the classroom.

Organization of Reform

In order to see the role of ethnographic research in schools from a perspective of empowerment, it is important to describe school reform. School reform is not intruded here to mean the prescribed code of behavior or actions for teachers or administrators by the decision-makers above them, whether these behaviors or actions are the result of formal evaluations, work by consultants or personal views of persons in power. Genuine school reform does not consist of coercive measures imposed on subordinates in the form of structural arrangements of management or of control over resources selectively available to subordinates. Because American schools are part of a democratic society, and because they are the key institution for the transmission of national cultural values, including democratic values, reform is usually accomplished by a combination of both pressures from decision makers and genuine commitment to change on the part of the persons involved (in this case teachers).

Ethnographic research can be instrumental in exploring the communication channels that serve the function of facilitating reform. Also ethnographic approaches can be effective in documenting the psychodynamics of change as pressures coming from above meet persuasion coming from the grassroots, resulting in a series of jointly made decisions by collectivities (e.g. the teachers) and their superiors (e.g. the superintendents).

There is one particular area where ethnographic research can serve the important purpose of helping decision makers understand the reasons behind successful change for the better, or resistance to change on the part of teachers and principals. This is the area of schools with culturally diverse student populations and a majority of White or mainstream teachers. The inter-ethnic conflict, the problems in communication, the clash of cultural values, and the resulting underachievement of ethnic/linguistically different student populations can be studied via ethnographic research methods more productively than with traditional methods of research borrowed from psychology or sociology — for example, with the use of correlational designs, questionnaires or quick interviews.

The nature and consequences of inter-ethnic conflict go back to the roots of cultural differences between ethnic communities and the school personnel. The surface analysis of such conflicts most frequently take the form of 'deficit' approaches to the study of ethnically diverse student achievement, and is guided by assumptions of serious limitations exhibited by ethnically different students, limitations that make it nearly impossible for teachers to teach successfully. Alternative explanations pursued in ethnographic studies examine the inability of school systems to capitalize on the cultural and linguistic resources of ethnically different children and communities, or the unwillingness to adopt more flexible curricular structures that permit ethnically different children to acquire 'required' knowledge gradually through less conventional methods, in recognition of their different experience and different cultural or linguistic backgrounds. The need to build into school activities some successful experiences for children who have just arrived seems to require genuine cultural sensitivity and understanding of the learning processes across cultures.

A long-term reform at the elementary or secondary school level that takes into account the role of language and culture must recognize the need to prepare teachers to recognize cultural diversity and to communicate effectively with diverse children. It seems that ultimately at the heart of any effective reform are teachers who are truly committed to the children's welfare, without prejudice toward those who are different or who are attempting to adjust to the new culture of the school and society. These teachers have the kind of experiences and understanding that permits them to interact effectively with their students, to anticipate their thoughts, their efforts to construct cognitive domains and make sense of text, their motivational responses and the overall intellectual investment they make in studying the subject matter.

Fundamentally, an ethnography of empowerment as

applied to school research recognizes the need to codify subject matter knowledge and to package it appropriately, but not at the expense of contextualization of knowledge. Teachers must know mathematics, or geography, or history or any other subject, as Shulman has suggested (1987a). Having the knowledge of subject matter is not enough. Teachers must also know what students know and how they will go from their knowledge base to the new context. As Sockett has stated:

> Shulman's concern with a development model of teachers as professionals moving toward codified wisdom-in-practice, and his rejection of tacit knowledge as lacking explanatory power for the public, suggest that his perspective on teaching, as an occupation incorporating an activity, is too much driven by the demands of public explicability and *assessment* ... Professionalization, Shulman is saying, demands an account of the knowledge base of teaching (Sockett, 1987:214–215).

Shulman answered by stressing the 'centrality of knowledge' and the 'predictability of schools', by suggesting that recent tendencies exist to discover the 'virtues of chaos and flux' among those who advocate ethnic, cultural or social diversity in schools (Shulman, 1987b:479).

The controversy points out the difficult nature of reform strategies. The predictability of schools is based on their ethnic or cultural homogeneity, which is rapidly disappearing in America. The need to provide a broad context of information prior to investing reform efforts in curriculum or instructional techniques is recognized by ethnographers.

In order to see the possible usages of an ethnography of empowerment in the context of schools from the perspective of the teachers, that is, focusing on the empowerment of teachers to teach culturally diverse students effectively, we will describe the ethnographic categories to be covered. These categories would apply to a school district, or a particular school, depending on the scope of the study. In any event, the study would be conceptualized as a long-term study (a minimum of three years).

Ethnographic Information on Schools

The following categories illustrate the various kinds of information intended to contextualize issues of cultural adjustment of ethnically different students and of mainstream teachers, as well as information intended to facilitate teachers' ability to organize the curriculum and instruction in order to facilitate students' productive participation in the learning process.

Ethnohistorical Data on School and Communities

Ethnohistorical information on school and communities is intended to provide understanding of the relative stability of school and community, their cultural roots, their congruent or conflicting cultures, and the patterns of exchanges between both. The following examples of types of information will show how reform can be better conceptualized after decision makers understand the ethnohistory of school and community:

1 Original founders, grow patterns, and ethnic membership as far back as historical records permit. What has been the relative mobility of students as they grow? Has the community been isolated, or in close connection with other communities? Have social, economic and historical factors changed the nature of the school and its ability to provide quality instruction for children?

2 Social and economic support systems on which the community and school were developed. Is the school placed in a mining town, or in a rich suburban area, or in a migrant camp? Is there a marked social, economic and cultural distance between town, camp or area in which the school is located, and the school personnel?

3 Relationships between school and community, between school personnel and student families, in a historical perspective. Have teachers and principals been commuters and outsiders to the members of the community? Has there been a radical change in community support of

teachers' work, and if so, what are the reasons for such a change?

Social and Cultural Environment of School

The current social and cultural environment of a school is elusive, intangible, and yet a most important indicator of vitality, high student achievement and genuine learning. If there are clear physical compartments separating different social or ethnic groups of students, and if there is a great deal of tension and conflict in the interaction between the various social or ethnic groups, it is likely that learning is jeopardized or prevented in school. Differential resource allocation and differential quality of instruction for the different social or ethnic groups in school is a clear sign that the learning climate in school is of poor quality. Ethnically, linguistically, socially or economically heterogeneous schools that resort to tracking, or to other ways of isolating the 'low achievers' and offering preferential treatment to the 'high achievers' conveys highly disruptive messages to all students. Such messages essentially destroy faith in human equality under the law and genuine respect for the cultures and values of other groups. Such school structural patterns disempower ethnic/ linguistically different students and prevent them from entering the educational system or from surviving in the system if they ever enter it. The following categories can give the reader an idea of the kind of information an ethnographer would look for:

1 Geographical location and physical appearance of school in comparison with other schools in the area. Is one school for Blacks, Hispanics or Asians, while another is primarily for Whites? Are the teachers and principal White and the student population culturally or linguistically different?

2 Physical appearance of offices and classrooms, decor, hygiene, access to students and outsiders, air and noise pollution levels, adequacy of materials and books, visual aids, etc. Specifically, are the classrooms and offices

clean, well decorated, open and conducive to learning activities?

3 Violence, interpersonal conflict, coercion or self-initiated discipline, cooperative arrangements or exclusive groupings, overall working climate. Are there, for example, obvious incidents of use of police to prevent violence, is the school fenced or the classroom locked to prevent the entrance of outsiders? Are students visibly engaged in violent conflicts? Are teachers and the principal spending much of their time in discipline matters?

Ethnic and Social Composition of the School

The ethnic composition and changes in school, as seen over a period of time, can show the presence of cultural conflicts and problems of school personnel in coping with the social and educational problems of children and young adults both at home and in school. The following types of information might help to explain why a long-term study of the ethnic and social composition of school personnel and student population is important for planning reform:

1 Trends of changes of student population's ethnic, economic and social backgrounds. The speed of the change and the proportions of the change are equally important, especially if these changes in student population contrast with the stability of white mainstream teachers and principals, or with a pattern of teacher burnout and short-term employment.

2 Changes over time in the relative stability of some student populations leading to inter-ethnic conflict situations. For example, has the increase of Black or Hispanic population been followed by a decrease (in absolute numbers) of White students? Or has the increase of low-income population been followed by the decrease of middle class ethnic and White? Is there a significant difference in the literacy levels of the low-income students and their families if compared with those of middle class?

Organizational Structure of School

There is a wide range of organizational arrangements in American schools, depending on local historical traditions, and the response to change on the part of school boards and communities. The degree of cohesiveness of school personnel, and the relative commitment of teachers and principal to school activities over a period of time are contingent upon the organizational models selected by superintendents and the rigor of the monitoring process established in school districts. There are also important differences in the assumptions that school administrators carry in their heads as they make important changes in policy and practice. Important issues to follow ethnographically over a period of time are the following:

1 Specific line of command, and the distribution of duties. Management styles, accessibility of decision makers and delegation of responsibilities. Monitoring systems and communication between managers and school personnel. More concretely, is there an adequate administrative structure and a clear understanding of the distribution of roles and responsibilities? Are the principal or vice-principal unable to manage the day-to-day school business?

2 Support given to administrators by school personnel, degree of harmony and predictability of processes. Specifically, is there a problem of morale among faculty, or among parents? Is the principal an effective manager? Is the principal fair, considerate and judicious in the use of his/her power? Is there a continuous crisis mode of operation, or is there a due process and relatively peaceful climate of functioning?

3 Administrative response to needed change and in the face of conflict. Is the principal or vice-principal capable of understanding and executing needed change? Can the principal play the role of intellectual leader in guiding teachers and parents through instructional changes and improvement processes? Is there sufficient stability in school administrators, or are they continuously being

175

changed? How is the school viewed by the superintendent vis-a-vis the other schools?

Teacher Profiles and Groupings

To know the teachers is to know the school. Even if the administration is not as good as it might be, if teachers are capable, responsible and committed to teach well, there is a good chance that problems can be resolved. Teachers are less and less able to stay on the job with full enthusiasm because their worth and rewards are neglected. Teacher problems have many aspects and manifest themselves in different ways. But it is important to see long-term trends in teacher mobility, change, or in patterns of stagnation and political retrenchment. The following categories can help if one is seeking historically grounded general information, and specific information over the last few years:

1 Teacher composition over the last three or five years. Ages, sex, background, residence, and assignments. Changes or stability in teachers in contrast to changes or stability in student population size or composition. Are there any patterns? Are these patterns explainable by administrative fiats, or community action, or how?

2 Teachers' views of their own lives and jobs. The internalization of the role in the context of recent unionization is particularly important. The resistance to change, or the willingness to invest in one's own professional development. The relative access some teachers have to support groups, in contrast with the isolation of other teachers.

3 Teachers' professional competence in subject matter as evidenced by the quality of their teaching and the involvement and learning by their students. Teachers' ability to work with culturally different children, and to communicate with them about subject matter. Overall cultural sensitivity of teachers. Is there evidence of prejudice about the possible talents of children of color? Are teachers aware of this prejudice? How do they deal with it?

Classroom Instruction

The information sought here deals with the nature of instructional activities, the organization of lessons, the performance of teachers, and the participation of students. Teachers' skills, their ability to learn and to transmit knowledge, their commitment to build students' confidence and achievement motivation, and other important attributes of good teachers, are demonstrated during instruction. What is important is to know the specifics of what good teachers do and how they keep up the good work, especially in culturally diverse classrooms. Here are some specific issues:

1. Actual organization of classroom activities, and choice of interactional styles which determine relative participation of students, their access to knowledge and motivation to learn. Are there consistent patterns in the class that the teacher does not see? Is there an effective, well planned and carefully crafted lesson? Does the teacher allow for a two-way communication or does s/he monopolize the floor without giving access to students to ask questions?

2. Teachers' awareness of the quality of their teaching, and of the outcomes of their teaching. Specifically, how do teachers feel about their teaching, and about the outcomes of their teaching? How do they prepare for their classes? Are they aware of what the children's experiences and backgrounds are? Can s/he use such experiences to communicate more effectively? Is the teacher aware of the potential support coming from parents to motivate students to achieve? Is she physically and mentally able to cope with the demands of the classroom?

Functional Adaptation of the Curriculum

As knowledge base and student population change the curriculum should to be adjusted and updated. To make the appropriate curriculum adaptation teachers are guided by administrators via workshops, classes in universities, experiments with new materials, and other mechanisms. The nature of these adaptations must recognize the cultural, linguistic and social changes in the student population. Each subject must be calibrated and the effectiveness of the curriculum tested by a number of means. An ethnographer can see patterns in the participation of teachers, and results in student participation and performance. No specific questions will be listed here because there are many and they are very diverse. Each subject at each level can raise a set of questions regarding appropriate preparation of students to engage meaningfully in a lesson. Bringing students into meaningful participation in order to continue to learn can prevent the repetitious experience of failure that ultimately disenfranchises many culturally and socially different children and young adults in American schools.

Students' Work and Play in School

The school seen from the perspective of students is quite a different reality from that seen from the teachers' or administrators' perspective. To know this perspective requires careful observation, interviews and continuous reflection. In the case of heterogeneous schools it is even more important to internalize the students' different perspectives of school that different students have. School experience can be highly oppressive and destructive from the students' point of view. In order to explore this reality, we need to ask students how they feel about teachers, peers, school activities, study, homework, the playground, and about themselves. Selective interviews with students and their families, observations in the home and in school, discussion with teachers, and other ethnographic techniques (including video- and audio-tape) can reveal patterns of the increasing isolation of students, deep depression, feelings of neglect and even despair. Students are often neglected until a crisis shows that it is too late to do anything. Increasing suicide rates in certain ethnic groups and social classes, lack of motivation to achieve and violence are manifestations of students' views of how dysfunctional schools are.

School-Community Relations

The study of school–community relations must include the reality of the families at home. We cannot wait until the parents come to knock on the school doors. The school must reach out and invest in the community, in the parents. The problem with trying to conduct a study of school–community relations is that often the community is no longer a community, or it has become a battleground for gangs and drug pushers, or it has become divided by class or ethnic boundaries to the point that there is no chance to engage in cooperative effort to support their school. But, in places where there is still time to make a difference, the school personnel should invest a great deal of time and resources in involving parents and in helping them help their own children.

Long-term Support for Reform

We must remind ourselves that if we do not protect our investment in the early years of school by creating adequate learning environments in elementary and secondary schools, children will not make it through the system to specialized graduate work and training, and consequently they will not be able to play a key role in the organization of future schools. Culturally, ethnically, socio-economically different and other ethnic/linguistically different children must find their way in the system if we want to retain our democratic structures and our technological place in the world.

Schools will continue to play a crucial role in the future of American democracy by providing quality instruction for all children, regardless of race, color, social class, family background or religion. A fundamental philosophical assumption guiding ethnographic research for empowerment is that all children can learn if taught well, that is, if taught in ways that recognize their linguistic, cultural or social background and experiences.

Ethnographic Information and Planned Interventions

With the above information it is possible to plan specific interventions, or the components of a long-term reform, intended to increase the quality of education for linguistic minorities and ensure of educational opportunities above elementary and secondary education.

Reform and innovation, coping with the world-wide problems created by incessant waves of immigrants in search of economic and cultural survival, are all in the hands of teachers and school personnel. But teachers and school personnel are in the hands of principals, superintendents, school boards, departments of education, state and federal agencies, and ultimately the citizenry. Educational reform without social reform is ineffective. Segregation and prejudice at home or in the community will find its way in school. Schools need support, resources and a strong backing from the administrators at all levels, all the way to the macro-structural levels of our government. The role of an ethnography for empowerment is to provide a realistic notion of how the social and cultural values of the larger society influence the organization of schools and the quality of instruction.

Bibliography

ALLEN, J., BARR, D., COCHRAN, M., DEAN, C. and GREENE, J. (1989) *Power and Empowerment*, Unpublished paper, College of Human Ecology, Cornell University Empowerment Project, Ithaca, NY.

AMERICAN COUNCIL ON EDUCATION (1986) *Minorities in Higher Education*, Washington, DC: Office of Minority Concerns, Fifth Annual Status Report.

APPLE, M. (1979) *Ideology and Curriculum*, London: Routledge and Kegan Paul.

BARR, D.J. (1989) *Critical Reflections on Power*, Cornell University Project, Department of Human Services Studies, College of Human Ecology, Ithaca, NY.

BARRY, H., CHILD, I.H. and BACON, M.K. (1959) 'Relation of childrearing to subsistence economy', *American Anthropologist*, **61**, pp. 51–63.

BATESON, G. (1972) 'Toward a theory of play and fantasy', in BATESON, G. (Ed.), *Steps to an Ecology of Mind*, New York: Ballantine, (reprinted from *A.P.A. Psychiatric Research Reports*, 1955, **II**)

BERNHEIMER, C.P., GALLIMORE, R. and WEISNER, T.S. (1989) *Ecocultural Theory as a Context for the Individual Family Service Plan*, Los Angeles, CA: University of California.

BLEICH, D. (1988) *The Double Perspective: Language Literacy and Social Relations,* New York: Oxford University Press.

BROWN, S.V. (1987) *Minorities in the Graduate Education Pipeline*, Princeton: Educational Testing Service.

BROWN, S.V. (1988) *Increasing Minority Faculty: An Elusive Goal*, A Research Report of the Minority Education Project, Graduate Record Examinations Board and Educational Testing Service, Princeton: Educational Testing Services.

CALIFORNIA STATE DEPARTMENT OF EDUCATION (1987) *A Student Population by Ethnicity*, Educational Demographics Unit, California State Department, Sacramento, CA.

CENTER FOR EDUCATION STATISTICS (1986) *The Condition of Education*, Washington, DC: US Government Printing Office.

COLE, M. (1985) 'The zone of proximal development: Where culture and cognition create each other', In WERTSCH, J.V. (Ed.), *Culture, Communication and Cognition: Vygotskian Perspectives*, Cambridge, MA: Cambridge University Press, pp. 146–61.

COLE, M. and D'ANDRADE, R. (1982) 'The influence of schooling on concept formation: Some preliminary conclusions', *The Quarterly Newsletter of the Laboratory of Comparative Human Cognition*, **4**(2), pp. 19–26.

COOK-GUMPERZ, J. (Ed.) (1986) *The Social Construction of Literacy*, Cambridge, MA: Cambridge University Press.

CONTRERAS, A.R. and DELGADO-CONTRERAS (in press) 'Mexican American parent involvement: A case study of first stage of school participation', in HARRIS III, J.J. and HELD, C. (Eds), *The State of Education in Pluralistic America*. Bloomington, IN: Indiana University Press.

CORTES, C.E. (1986) 'The education of language minority students: A contextual interaction model', in BILINGUAL EDUCATION OFFICE (Ed.), *Beyond Language: Social and Cultural Factors in Schooling Language Minority Students*, Los Angeles, CA: Evaluation, Dissemination, and Assessment Center, pp. 3–34.

CUMMINS, J. (1981) 'The role of primary language development in promoting educational success for language minority students', in *Schooling and Language Minority Students: A Theoretical Framework*, Los Angeles, CA: California State University at Los Angeles Evaluation, Dissemination and Assessment Center, pp. 3–49.

CUMMINS, J. (1984) *Heritage Language Education: A Literature Review*, Toronto CAN: Ministry of Education, Ontario.

CUMMINS, J. (1986) 'Empowering minority students: A framework for intervention', *Harvard Educational Review*, **56**(1), pp. 18–35.

CUMMINS, J. (1989) *Empowering Minority Students*, Paper presented at the California Association for Bilingual Education, Sacramento, CA, January.

DAVEY, E. and DAVEY, W. (1988) *The History of Redwood City*, Document presented to the Redwood City Council as part of the Community Service Program.

DE AVILA, E. (1986) *Motivation, Intelligence and Access: A Theoretical Framework for the Education of Minority Language. Students Issues in English Language Development*, Washington, DC National Clearinghouse for Bilingual Education, pp. 21–31.

DELGADO-GAITAN, C. (1983) *Learning How: Rules for Knowing and Doing for Mexican Children at Home, Play, and School*, Doctoral dissertation, Stanford, CA: Stanford University.

DELGADO-GAITAN, C. (1987) 'Mexican adult literacy: New directions for immigrants,' in GOLDMAN, S. and TRUEBA, H.T. (Eds), *Becoming Literate in English as a Second Language*, Norwood, NJ: Ablex, pp. 9–32.

DELGADO-GAITAN, C. (1988a) 'Sociocultural adjustment to school and academic achievement', *Journal of Early Adolescence*, **8**, pp. 63–82.

DELGADO-GAITAN, C. (1988b) 'The value of conformity: Learning to stay in school', *Anthropology and Education Quarterly*, **19**, pp. 354–81.

DELGADO-GAITAN, C. (1990) *Literacy for Empowerment: The Role of Parents in Children's Education*, Basingstoke, England: Falmer Press.

DEVOS, G. (1967) 'Essential elements of caste; Psychological determinants in structural theory,' in DEVOS, A. and WAGATSUMA, H. (Eds), *Japan's Invisible Race: Caste in Culture and Personality*, Berkeley, CA: University of California Press, pp. 332–84.

DEVOS, G. (1973) 'Japan's outcastes: The problem of the

Burakumin', in B. WHITAKER (Ed.), *The Fourth World: Victims of Group Oppression*, New York: Schocken Books, pp. 307–27.

DEVOS, G. (1978) 'Selective permeability and reference group sanctioning: Psychocultural continuities in role degradation', in YINGER, M. and CUTLER, S. (Eds), *Major Social Issues*, New York: Free Press, pp. 7–24.

DEVOS, G. (1980) 'Ethnic adaptation and minority status', *Journal of Cross-Cultural Psychology*, **11**, pp. 101–24.

DEVOS, G. (1982) 'Adaptive strategies in US minorities', in E.E. JONES and S.J. KORCHIN (Eds), *Minority Mental Health* New York: Praeger, pp. 74–117.

DEVOS, G. (1983) 'Ethnic identity and minority status: Some psycho-cultural considerations', in JACOBSON-WIDDING, A. (Ed.), *Identity: Personal and Sociocultural*, Uppsala: Almquist Wiksell Trycheri Ab, pp. 90–113.

DEVOS, G. (1984) 'Ethnic persistence and role degradation: An illustration from Japan', Paper read at the American Soviet Symposium on Contemporary Ethnic Processes in the USA and USSR, New Orleans, LA, April.

DEVOS, G. (1988) *Differential Minority Achievement in Cross Cultural Perspective; The Case of Korean in Japan and the United States*, Paper presented at the American Anthropological Association Meetings, Phoenix, AZ, November.

DEVOS, G. and WAGATSUMA, H. (1966) *Japan's Invisible Race: Caste in Culture and Personality*, Berkeley, CA: University of California Press.

DIAZ, S., MOLL, L. and MEHAN, H. (1986) 'Sociocultural resources in instruction: A context-specific approaches', in BILINGUAL EDUCATION OFFICE (Ed.), *Beyond Language: Social and Cultural Factors in Schooling Language Minority Students*, Los Angeles, CA: Evaluation, Dissemination, and Assessment Center, pp. 187–230.

DIXON, C. and NESSEL, D. (1983) *Language Experience Approach to Reading and Writing*, Hayward, CA: The Alemany Press.

DUNN, L.M. (1987) *Bilingual Hispanic Children on the US Mainland: A Review of Research on Their Cognitive, Linguistic, and Scholastic Development*, Circle Pines, MN: American Guidance Service.

ERICKSON, F. (1984) 'School literacy, reasoning, and civility: An anthropologist's perspective', *Review of Educational Research*, **54**(4), pp. 525–544.

EVANS, J.W., WALD, M.S., SMREKAR, C. and VENTRESCA, M.J. (1989) 'A sociographic portrait', in KIRST, M. (Ed.), *Conditions of Children in California*, Berkeley, CA: University of California, PACE, pp. 13–25.

FERNANDEZ, R.M., PALSEN, R. and HIRANO-NAKANISHI, M. (1989) 'Dropping out among Hispanic Youth', *Social Science Research*, 18 pp. 21–52.

FISHER, J. and FISHER, A. (1963) 'The New Englander of Orchard Town, USA', in B. WHITING (Ed.), *Six Cultures: Studies of Child Rearing*, New York: John Wiley.

FISHMAN, J. (1976) *Bilingual Education: An International Sociological Perspective*, Rowley, MA: Newbury House.

FRAKE, C. (1964) 'Notes on queries in ethnography', *American Anthropologist*, **66**(3), pp. 132–45.

FREIRE, P. (1970) *Pedagogy of the Oppressed*, New York: Continuum.

FREIRE, P. and MACEDO, D. (1987) *Reading the Word and the World*. South Hadley, MA: Bergin and Garvey.

GILMORE, P. and GLATTHORN, A.A. (1982) *Children In and Out of School: Ethnography and Education*, Washington, DC: Center for Applied Linguistics.

GOODENOUGH, W.H. (1976) 'Multiculturalism as the normal human experience', *Anthropology and Education Quarterly*, **7**(4), pp. 4–7.

GOODMAN, K.S. (1986) *What's Whole in Whole Language*, Portsmouth, NH: Heinemann.

GOTTLIEB, E.E. and LA BELLE, T.J. (1990) 'Ethnographic contextualization of Freire's Discourse: Consciousness raising theory and practice', *Anthropology and Education Quarterly*, **21**(1), pp. 3–18.

GRANT, C.A. and SLEETER, C.E. (1986) 'Race, class and gender in education research: An argument for integrative analysis', *Review of Educational Research*, **56**, pp. 195–211.

GREENE, M. (1986) 'In search of a critical pedagogy', *Harvard Educational Review*, **56**(4), pp. 427–41.

GRIFFIN, H. (1984) 'The coordination of meaning in the creation of a shared make-believe reality', in BRETHERTON, I. (Ed.), *Symbolic Play*, New York: Academic Press, pp. 73–96.

GUMPERZ, J. (1986) 'Interactional sociolinguistics in the study of schooling', in COOK-GUMPERZ, J. (Ed.), *The Social Construction of Literacy*, Cambridge, MA: Cambridge University Press, pp. 45–68.

GUMPERZ, J. and HYMES, D. (Eds) (1964) 'The ethnography of communication', *American Anthropologist*, **66**(6).

GUMPERZ, J., and HYMES, D. (Eds) (1972) *Directions in Sociolinguistics: The Ethnography of Communication*, New York: Holt, Rinehart, and Winston.

HAKUTA, K. (1986) *The Mirror of Language*, New York: Basic Books.

HALFON, N., JAMESON, W., BRINDIS, C., LEE, P.R., NEWACHECK, P.W., KORENBROT, C., McCROSKEY, J. and ISMAN, R. (1989) 'Health', in M. KIRST (Ed.), *Conditions of Children in California*, Berkeley, CA: University of California, PACE, pp. 143–201.

HATTON, E. (1989) 'Levi-Strauss's *Bricolage* and Theorizing Teachers' Work', *Anthropology and Education Quarterly* **20**(2), pp. 74–96.

HEATH, S.B. (1983) *Ways with Words*, Cambridge, MA: Cambridge University Press.

HERNANDEZ-CHAVEZ, E. (1984) 'The inadequacy of English immersion education as an educational approach for language minority students in the United States', in *Studies on Immersion Education*, Sacramento, CA: California State Department of Education, pp. 144–83.

HORNBERGER, N. (1988) 'Iman Chay?: Quechua children in Peru's schools', in H. TRUEBA and C. DELGADO-GAITAN (Eds), *School and Society: Teaching Content Through Culture*, New York: Praeger, pp. 99–117.

KIRST, M. (Ed.) (1989) *Conditions of Children in California*, Berkeley, CA: Policy Analysis for California Education, pp. 13–35.

KOHN, M. (1967) 'Social class and parent-child relationships: An interpretation', in R. COSER (Ed.), *Life Cycle and Achievement in America*, New York: Harper and Row, pp. 21–42.

KOHN, M. (1983) 'On the transmission of values in the family:

A preliminary formulation', in A.C. KERCKHOFF (Ed.), *Research in Sociology of Education and Socialization*, Greenwich, CT: JAI Press, pp. 3–12.

KRASHEN, S. and TERRELL, T.D. (1983) *The Natural Approach*, New York: Pergamon.

LEACOCK, E.B. (1969) *Teaching and Learning in City Schools*, New York: Basic Books.

LEVI-STRAUSS, C. (1966) *The Savage Mind*, Chicago, IL: The University of Chicago Press.

MCDERMOTT, R. (1977) 'Social relations as contexts for learning in school,' *Harvard Educational Review*, **47**(2), pp. 198–213.

MCDERMOTT, R. (1987a) 'Achieving school failure: An anthropological approach to illiteracy and social stratification', in G. SPINDLER (Ed.), *Education and Cultural Process: Anthropological Approaches*, (2nd ed.), Prospects Heights, IL: Waveland Press, Inc., pp. 173–209.

MCDERMOTT, R. (1987b) 'The explanation of minority school failure, again', *Anthropology and Education Quarterly*, **18**, pp. 361–4.

MCLAUGHLIN, B. (1985) *Second-Language Acquisition in Childhood: Volume 2. School-Age Children*, Hillsdale, NJ: Lawrence Erlbaum Associates.

MEAD, G.H. (1967) *Mind, Self, and Society*. Chicago, IL: University Chicago Press, (Originally published, 1934).

MEAD, M. (1943) 'Our educational emphases in primitive perspective', *American Journal of Sociology*, **48**, 633–9.

MEHAN, H. (1984) 'Language and schooling', *Sociology of Education*, **57**, pp. 174–83.

MINNIS, D. (1989) *Financial Support for Graduate Students*, Unpublished manuscript, Davis, CA, University of of California, Graduate Division.

NATIONAL RESEARCH COUNCIL (1986) *Summary Report 1985: Doctorate Recipients from United States Universities*, Washington, D.C. National Academy Press.

NICHOLS, P.C. (1989) 'Storytelling in Carolina: Continuities and contrasts', *Anthropology and Education Quarterly*, **20**(3) pp. 232–45.

OGBU, J. (1974) *The Next Generation: An Ethnography of Education in an Urban Neighborhood*, New York: Academic Press.

Bibliography

OGBU, J. (1978) *Minority Education and Caste: The American System in Cross-cultural Perspective*, New York: Academic Press.

OGBU, J. (1981) 'Origins of human competence: A cultural-ecological perspective', *Child Development*, **52**, pp. 413–29.

OGBU, J. (1982) 'Cultural discontinuities and schooling', *Anthropology and Education Quarterly*, **13**(4), pp. 290–307.

OGBU, J. (1987) 'Variability in minority responses to schooling: Nonimmigrants vs. immigrants', in G. SPINDLER and L. SPINDLER (Eds), *Interpretive Ethnography of Education: At Home and Abroad*, Hillsdale, NJ: Lawrence Erlbaum Associates, pp. 255–78.

ORTIZ, F.I. (1988) 'Hispanic-American children's experiences in classrooms: A comparison between Hispanic and non-Hispanic children', in L. WEIS (Ed.), *Class, Race, and Gender in American Education*, Albany, NY: State University of New York Press, pp. 63–86.

PHILIPS, S. (1983) *The Invisible Culture: Communication in Classroom and Community on the Warm Springs Indian Reservation*, New York: Longman.

RAPPAPORT, J. (1981) 'In praise of paradox: A social policy of empowerment overprevention', *American Journal of Community Studies*, **9**(1), pp. 1–25.

RODRIGUEZ, R. (1982) *Hunger of Memory: The Education of Richard Rodriguez*, New York: Bantam Books.

ROUSE, R.C. (1989) *Mexican Migration to the United States: Family Relations in the Development of a Transnational Migrant Circuit*, Unpublished doctoral dissertation, Stanford, CA: Stanford University.

RUEDA, R. (1987) 'Social and communicative aspects of language proficiency in low-achieving language minority students', in H. TRUEBA (Ed.), *Success or Failure: Linguistic Minority Children at Home and in School*, New York: Harper and Row, pp. 185–97.

RUEDA, R. and MEHAN, H. (1988) 'Metacognition and passing: Strategic interaction in the lives of students with learning disabilities', *Anthropology and Education Quarterly*, **17**(3), pp. 139–65.

RUMBERGER, R.W. (1990) 'Chicano Dropouts', Chapter to

appear in R.R. VALENCIA (Ed.) *Chicano School Failure and Success: Research and Policy Agendas for the 1990's*, Basingstoke, England: Falmer Press.

SEGURA, D. (1989) 'Chicano and Mexican immigrant women at work: The impact of class, race and gender on occupational mobility', *Gender and Society*, **3**(1), pp. 37–52.

SHULMAN, L. (1987a) 'Knowledge and teaching: Foundations of the new reform', *Harvard Educational Review*, **57**(1) pp. 1–22.

SHULMAN, L. (1987b) 'Sounding an alarm: A reply to Sockett', *Harvard Educational Review*, **57**(4), pp. 473–82.

SOCKETT, H. (1987) 'Has Shulman got the strategy right?' *Harvard Educational Review*, **57**(2), pp. 208–19.

SOLOMON, B. (1976) *Black Empowerment*. New York: Columbia University Press.

SPINDLER, G. (1963) *Education and Culture: Anthropological Approaches*, New York: Holt, Rinehart and Winston.

SPINDLER, G. (1974) 'The transmission of American culture', In G. SPINDLER (Ed.) *Education and Culture: Anthropological Approaches*, New York: Holt, Rinehart and Winston, pp. 279–310.

SPINDLER, G. (1982) *Doing the Ethnography of Schooling: Educational Anthropology in Action*, New York: Holt, Rinehard and Winston.

SPINDLER, G. (1987) 'The transmission of culture', In G.D. SPINDLER (Ed.), *Education and Cultural Process: Anthropological Approaches* (2nd ed.), Prospect Heights, IL: Waveland Press, pp. 303–34.

SPINDLER, G. and SPINDLER, L. (1989) 'There are no dropouts among the Arunta and Hutterites', in TRUEBA, H., SPINDLER, G., SPINDLER, L. (Eds) *What Do Anthropologists Have to Say About Dropouts?* Basingstoke, England: Falmer Press, pp. 7–15.

SPINDLER G. and SPINDLER, L. (1990) *The American Cultural Dialogue and its Transmission*, Basingstoke, England: Falmer Press.

SUÁREZ-OROSCO, M. (1987) 'Towards a psycho-social understanding of Hispanic adaptation to American schooling', in TRUEBA, H.T. (Ed.), in *Success or Failure? Learning and the*

Language Minority Student, Cambridge, MA: Newbury House, pp. 156–68.

SUÁREZ-OROZCO, M. (1989) *Central American Refugees and US High Schools: A Psychosocial Study of Motivation and Achievement*, Stanford, CA: Stanford University Press.

THARP, R. and GALLIMORE, R. (1989) *Rousing Minds to Life: Teaching, Learning and Schooling in Social Context*, Cambridge, MA: Cambridge University Press.

TRUEBA, H. (1983) 'Adjustment problems of Mexican American children: An anthropological study', *Learning Disabilities Quarterly*. **6**(4), pp. 395–415.

TRUEBA, H. (1987) 'Organizing classroom instruction in specific sociocultural contexts: Teaching Mexican youth to write in English', in S. GOLDMAN and H. TRUEBA (Eds), *Becoming Literate in English as a Second Language: Advances in Research and Theory*, Norwood, NJ: Ablex, pp. 235–52.

TRUEBA, H. (1988a) 'Peer socialization among minority students: A high school dropout prevention program', in H. TRUEBA and C. DELGADO-GAITAN (Eds), *School and Society: Learning Content Through Culture*, New York: Praeger Publishers, pp. 201–17.

TRUEBA, H. (1988b) 'English literacy acquisition: From cultural trauma to learning disabilities in minority students', *Linguistics and Education* **1**, pp. 125–52.

TRUEBA, H. (1988c) 'Culturally-based explanations of minority students' academic achievement', *Anthropology and Education Quarterly*, **19**(3), pp. 270–87.

TRUEBA, H.T. (1988d) 'Comments on L.M. Dunn's Bilingual Hispanic children on the US mainland: A review of research on their cognitive, linguistic and scholastic development', in a special issue of *Hispanic Journal of Behavioral Sciences*, **10**(3), pp. 253–62.

TRUEBA, H. (1989) *Raising Silent Voices: Educating the Linguistic Minorities for the 21st century*, New York: Harper and Row.

TRUEBA, H. (1990) 'The role of culture in literacy acquisition: An interdisciplinary approach to qualitative research', *International Journal of Qualitative Studies in Education*, **3**, pp. 1–13.

TRUEBA, H. and DELGADO-GAITAN, C. (Eds) (1988) *School and*

Society: Learning Content Through Culture, New York: Praeger Publishers.

TRUEBA, H., JACOBS, L. and KIRTON, E. (1990) *Cultural Conflict and Adaptation: The Case of Hmong Children in American Society*, Basingstoke, England: Falmer Press.

TRUEBA, H., SPINDLER, G. and SPINDLER, L. (Eds) (1990) *What Do Anthropologists Have to Say about Dropping Out?* Basingstoke, England: Falmer Press.

UNIVERSITY OF CALIFORNIA OFFICE OF THE PRESIDENT (1989a) *A Reference Guide for Student Affirmative Action Efforts at the University of California*, Admissions and Outreach Services, Berkeley, CA: University of California Press.

UNIVERSITY OF CALIFORNIA OFFICE OF THE PRESIDENT (1989b) *The Forces Influencing College Student Persistence: A Review of the Literature*, Student Research and Operations, Berkeley, CA: University of California Press.

UNIVERSITY OF CALIFORNIA OFFICE OF THE PRESIDENT (1989c) *Early Academic Outreach Program: Challenges and Opportunities Student Affirmative Action*, Admissions and Outreach Services, Berkeley, CA: University of California Press.

US BUREAU OF THE CENSUS (1988) *Hispanic Population of the United States: March 1987*, Current Population Reports, Series p–20, No. 426, Washington, DC: US Government Printing Office.

VYGOTSKY, L.S. (1978) *Mind in Society: The Development of Higher Psychological Processes*, M. COLE, V. JOHN-TEINER, S. SCRIBNER, and E. SOUBERMAN, (Eds and Trans), Cambridge, MA: Harvard University Press.

WAGATSUMA, H. and DEVOS, G. (1984) *Heritage of Endurance: Family Patterns and Delinquency Formation in Urban Japan*, Berkeley, CA: University of California Press.

WALD, M.S., EVANS, J.W., SMREKAR, C. and VENTRESCA, M.J. (1989) 'Family life', in M.W. KIRST (Ed.), *Conditions of Children in California*, Berkeley, CA: Policy Analysis for California Education, pp. 27–44.

WERTSCH, J. (1985) *Vygotsky and the Social Formation of the Mind*, Cambridge, MA: Harvard University Press.

Index

BELOIT COLLEGE LIBRARY

0 20 22 0040870 8

305.23
D378c